A Publication of the
Institute of Industrial Relations
University of California

Working-Class Suburb

A Study of Auto Workers in Suburbia

Bennett M. Berger

University of California Press

Berkeley, Los Angeles, London 1971

UNIVERSITY OF CALIFORNIA PRESS

BERKELEY AND LOS ANGELES

UNIVERSITY OF CALIFORNIA PRESS, LTD.

LONDON, ENGLAND

© 1960 BY

THE REGENTS OF THE UNIVERSITY OF CALIFORNIA

FOURTH PRINTING, 1971

ISBN: 0-520-00108-7 (CLOTH)

0-520-00109-5 (PAPER)

LIBRARY OF CONGRESS CATALOG CARD NUMBER 68-26522

PRINTED IN THE UNITED STATES OF AMERICA

Working-Class Suburb

Preface

During the last weekend of February, 1955, the Ford Division of the Ford Motor Company closed its assembly plant in Richmond, California, and moved, taking virtually all of its employees with it, to a brand new plant some fifty miles away in a town called Milpitas, a semirural community a few miles north of San Jose. As part of a larger study of some of the social and economic consequences of the move,[1] it was my job to conduct a survey of the Ford workers with a view toward discovering what changes in their lives and those of their families might be attributed to the move. In selecting a sample, I discovered that there were large concentrations of workers living in new tract suburbs which had been built not far from the plant. Driving through these tracts, I was immediately struck by the image of "suburbia," and an interview schedule was designed based upon the general assumption that these erstwhile urban working-class families, most of whom had lived in the drab industrial city of Richmond, would be learning middle-class behavior, beliefs, and aspirations as a result of the suburbanization process. It did not take very many interviews, however, to see that this assumption was mistaken. In spite of their "suburban" context, these families

[1] Undertaken by Professor John T. Wheeler of the School of Business Administration of the University of California, Berkeley.

were apparently unaffected to any great extent by the process whose existence I had hypothesized.

Until 1941 Richmond had been a small industrial town of about 25,000 persons, supported primarily by the big Standard Oil refinery which had been there since shortly after the turn of the century, and by a number of smaller industries including the local Ford plant which began production in 1931. With the outbreak of World War II, Richmond became a boom town. The opening of the Kaiser shipyards there attracted thousands of depression-dispossessed farmers from the Midwest and the South —especially from Arkansas and Oklahoma. This fact is reflected in the interviews because most of these depression migrants remained in Richmond or the Bay area after the war, and were absorbed by its industries—among which was the Ford company.

Between 1941 and 1943 Richmond's population quadrupled, and the Federal Government stepped in to construct row upon row of barracks-like emergency housing. The immense civic and housing problems which this population explosion engendered— problems which continued long after the end of the war—cannot be gone into here; in any case, they have been dealt with elsewhere.[2] I mention them only to point to the fact that many of our respondents came to Richmond during this wartime period, and that most of them at one time or another lived in this low-rent emergency housing; 38 per cent of our respondents were *still* living in these substandard government apartments in February, 1955, when the plant moved.

Although reference will continually be made to "the sample," the group that I interviewed is closer to a sort of specialized total population than it is to a sample. This is due to the method by which the respondents were selected. The suburb to be studied was selected first, and this selection was made on the basis of previous knowledge that it was heavily populated by Ford workers. Next, the name of every Ford worker residing in the tract was taken from the San Jose city directory. But since many of these people so selected were new employees, that is, people who had never worked in the Richmond plant, the list of names

---

[2] See Raymond Paul de Romanett, "Public Action and Community Planning: A Study in the Redevelopment of Richmond, California."

was checked against the local union's seniority list, and those whose seniority postdated the movement of the plant were eliminated. In this way the names of approximately 120 Ford workers, who had worked in the Richmond plant and consequently were new to the San Jose suburban tract, were gathered. Each of these persons received a letter informing him of the intent of the study and asking his coöperation; follow-up telephone calls were used to schedule appointments for interviews. Refusals, vacations, failures to keep appointments, and turnover reduced the list of names to 100, so that our "sample" really constitutes something very close to a total population of Ford workers residing in the tract studied. Since the tract is much like others in the same area—just beyond the eastern city limits of San Jose, near the base of the hills that rise to form the eastern wall of the industrially booming Santa Clara valley—there is little reason to doubt that many of the findings of the study would also apply to other new suburbs of booming Western cities which are populated primarily by well-paid workers in heavy industry. At the same time, it should be recognized that this is a study of a particular group of Ford workers—those who had moved from Richmond to a suburban tract near San Jose. Not all the findings would necessarily apply to similar samples of Ford workers in other tracts, to other samples of auto workers living in suburbs, or to all working-class suburbs.

All interviewing was in August and September, 1957, in the homes of the respondents, usually between 4:30 and 9:00 P.M. Each interview lasted approximately one hour. Although an interview schedule was used (see Appendix II), some freedom was taken with the wording of questions in order to minimize stiltedness and to maximize the natural flow of information. Every attempt was made to include as many members of the family as possible in the interview. In most of the interviews the wives participated directly. Where the wives were present, they themselves answered the questions having to do with their experience; where they were not present, the husbands reported the information for them, but no distinction between these two types of answers is made in the tables reporting this information. In those few cases where a question set off a family dispute, the response of the husband was recorded for statistical purposes, but the responses of other members of the family were also noted. In this connection we should state immediately that the wives and the adolescent children of the Ford workers seem, on the whole, considerably more status-conscious than the men and, since women tend to be style leaders in the suburbs, there is a possibility that our statistical tables, which report primarily the responses of the men, may understate the extent to which these working-class people are taking on middle-class style.

One other clarification should be made. The study has a comparative dimension in the sense that many of the questions were specifically designed to elicit answers comparing the respondents' experience before the move with their present experience as suburbanites. It should be kept in mind, however, that responses about experience before the move are *retrospective,* and may be colored by this fact. It might have been better to do two studies, one before and one after the move. But in the absence of that possibility, the retrospective data seem better than none at all.

One final caveat: Some may argue that the survey was premature, that two or two and a half years is not enough time for the impact of the suburban experience to make itself felt, and that consequently the apparent failure of most of our respondents to take on many of the characteristics commonly associated with "suburbia" is owing simply to the relatively brief span of time that they have lived in the suburb. Quite clearly, it *is* possible that out of this suburban crucible a middle-class style of life may *eventually* emerge. But the nature of the population suggests that this eventuality is likely to take a generation or so to develop—if, indeed, it should at all. Even this possibility may be negatively affected by developments (such as the possibility of the bright, new suburb turning into a suburban slum) which at this time it is not possible to predict. In the meantime, the 26-month average length of residence in the tract by our respondents seems a substantial enough piece of time for some of the newness of the experience to have rubbed off on them.

Looking a little more deeply into the backgrounds of these suburbanites, we find information that goes a long way toward suggesting the reasons that they have not developed, to any appreciable extent, a middle-class way of life—reasons which also suggest the implausibility of any such development in the near future. For one thing, 54 per cent were born on farms; only 14 per cent were born in metropolitan areas with populations greater than 100,000. Although 23 per cent report having been *raised* in cities, 58 per cent were raised on farms or in small villages of less than 2,500 population, and 6 per cent are foreign born. Of these suburbanites, 74 per cent have something less than a full high school education, 39 per cent never went beyond the eighth grade, and only 7 per cent reported education beyond high school graduation.

Although our sample shows a very heavy representation of persons from Arkansas and Oklahoma, our respondents come from 27 states representing all sections of the United States including Hawaii, and six foreign countries. In addition, the overwhelming majority of our respondents come from rural farm or working-class backgrounds. Forty-four per cent of their fathers were farmers, 21 per cent common laborers, and 22 per cent skilled laborers or foremen. Eighty-seven per cent of the respondents have never had a full-time, white-collar job. Nevertheless, they are virtually all homeowners.[3]

If it were a predominantly young group (as residents of suburbs are supposed to be), there might be some probability of these working-class suburbanites changing their basic living patterns; but it is not a predominantly young group.[4] The age spread forms a very nearly normal curve; there are as many in the 35- to 44-year-old age group as there are in the 25- to 34-year-old group, and there is a quite sizable percentage (39 per cent) who are more than 40. Correlated with the age spread of the group is, of course, the ages of their children, who run the gamut from infancy to childhood to adolescence to adulthood, marriage, and children of their own.

---

[3] I say "virtually" because one respondent, a widower, lives with his father, a retired Ford worker who owns the tract house in which they both live. Homeownership before the move was 31 per cent. In the suburb it is 99 per cent.

[4] The question of which age groups are best representative of "suburbia" is a question that can be resolved only by further research. Certainly there are good reasons for believing that young couples with small children seek the suburbs. On the other hand, our sample indicates that the charms of suburbs go beyond their alleged desirability as a place to raise children.

Table 1.1 rounds out a description of the sample that was interviewed. In all the following tables, N equals 100.

TABLE 1.1

CHARACTERISTICS OF THE SAMPLE
(*Percentages*)

AGE	
20-24	2
25-29	20
30-34	19
35-39	20
40-44	18
45-49	13
50-54	2
55-59	4
60 plus	2
Total	100

PLACE OF BIRTH	
Metropolitan area	14
Small city	15
Town (less than 2500 population)	11
Farm	54
Foreign	6
Total	100

EDUCATION (Last Grade Completed)	
1-6	8
7-8	31
9-11	35
12	19
12 plus trade school	1
college (non-graduate)	6
Total	100

(*Table 1.1 Continued*)

MARITAL STATUS

Married.	96
Single.	1
Widowed.	1
Divorced or separated.	2
Total.	100

NUMBER OF CHILDREN

0.	11
1.	19
2.	28
3.	28
4.	12
5.	2
Total.	100

RELIGION

Catholic.	23
"Protestant"[a]	23
Baptist.	22
Methodist.	4
Lutheran.	6
Mormon.	4
Church of Christ.	3
Presbyterian.	2
Other Protestants.	6
No religion.	7
Total.	100

JOB

Skilled.	9
Semiskilled, line.	50
Semiskilled, off line.	26
Foreman.	12
Other.	3
Total.	100

[a] No denomination given.

(Table 1.1 Continued)

LENGTH OF TIME WITH FORD (In Years)

1-5	34
6-10	22
11-15	32
16-20	7
21-25	2
26-30	2
31 plus	1
Total	100

FATHER'S OCCUPATION

Farmer	44
Unskilled and semiskilled laborer	21
Skilled worker, foreman	22
Sales	1
Small business	5
Professional or semiprofessional	2
Clerical	5
Total	100

INCOME (Weekly Take-Home Pay,Including Wife's, If Any)

$70-79	8
80-89	32
90-99	20
100-124	13
125-149	18
150 plus	9
Total	100

Although this study bears the name of a single author, no work of this kind is completed, or even gets under way, without a great deal of help. To Professor John T. Wheeler I owe thanks for having introduced me to the problem treated here, and for having read the manuscript with a sharp critical eye, especially for statistical tables. Professor William Kornhauser read the early drafts with the ruthless blue pencil and the thoroughgoing criticism for which he is both feared and admired by his students. I have profited from conversations with William Friedland, Nathan Glazer, and Martin Trow. Arnold Callan, of the subregional office of the United Automobile Workers, and Philip Buskirk, of the American Friends Service Committee, took time from their busy schedules to discuss the local situation with me and to help with the selection of the sample.

The coöperation and the financial support provided by the Institute of Industrial Relations were instrumental in making the study. Mrs. Margaret S. Gordon, the Associate Director of the Institute, and Stanford Seidner, of the Institute's statistical staff, deserve a special vote of thanks. Hanan Selvin gave me important advice at a crucial stage of the revision of the manuscript.

To Professor Reinhard Bendix I owe more than a formal acknowledgment can convey. Teacher, mentor, collaborator, colleague, cautious friend, he encouraged me when I was depressed, and disciplined my hurried impulses toward the facile phrase and the large generalization. Much of whatever theoretical grasp this work has is attributable to my training under him.

To my wife, Jean, goes my gratitude for accepting, at a difficult time, the tedious task of typing the manuscript.

Finally, this study belongs to the respondents who in a sense made it. One wonders what would happen to research in the social sciences if some dark god commanded people to refuse to be interviewed! To the 100 families who made the interviewing a pleasant as well as an illuminating experience, this study is dedicated. Let them be admitted to the anonymous and ghostly company of Heroes of Research.

Bennett M. Berger

University of Illinois,
Urbana

I originally undertook the study reported in this book because I thought I would be able to observe the transformation of a group of automobile assembly line workers (and their families) into the "suburbanites" who had become stock figures in American popular culture in the 1950's through the satirical and straight efforts of a variety of popular magazines. It seemed to me that, having found a working-class population more than two years settled in a new suburb, I was provided with an almost natural experimental setting in which to document the processes through which "suburbia" was supposed to exercise its profound and diffuse influence in transforming a group of mostly poorly educated and semi-skilled factory workers into those model middle class Americans obsessed with the problems of crabgrass and "conformity."

Well, it is now a matter of public record that my basic assumption was wrong. As the interview evidence piled up, it became clear that the lives of the suburbanites I was studying had not been profoundly affected in any statistically identifiable or sociologically interesting way. But I was cautious in the general inferences I drew. (While writing the book I remember the sign I put on the wall over my desk; it read: "Remember: ritual caution.") The study was based on only one small sample, of one suburb, of one metropolitan area, in one region, and it suffered from all of the methodological limitations inherent in small case studies. Its results were sufficiently clear, however, to enable me to question the right of others to generalize freely about "suburbia" on the basis of very few studies of selected suburbs which happened to be homogeneously middle or upper middle class in character —especially when it seemed apparent that suburban housing was increasingly available to all but the lowest income levels and status groups.

The research that has been done on suburbs in the years since

I did my own has given me no reason to alter the conclusions I drew then; it has, in fact, strengthened them. Samuel Kaplan helped enormously by undertaking in 1964 a replication of my own study, which largely confirmed its major findings. But in addition to Kaplan's work, we now have access to S. D. Clark's survey of a variety of suburbs around Toronto and Herbert Gans' monumental study of predominantly lower-middle-class Levittown, New Jersey, as well as to smaller studies, for example, Scott Greer's study of a Negro suburb of St. Louis, Walter's and Wirt's study of Cleveland suburbs, and the studies of William Dobriner and John Liell of Levittown, New York—Liell's work being the first I know of to study a suburb over a substantial period of time, first in 1951, shortly after its founding, and again in 1960. Now, the big survey research centers are going beyond case studies to generalizations about suburbia based upon the study of national samples of population analyzed in terms of place of residence.[1]

None of this research can be expected to give much comfort to those who find it convenient to believe that living in suburbs exercises some mysterious power over its residents to transform them into replicas of Whyte's practitioners of "The Outgoing Life." There seems to be increasing consensus among students of suburbs that suburban development is simply the latest phase of a process of urban growth that has been going on for a long time, that the cultural character of suburbs varies widely in terms of the social make-up of its residents, and the personal and group

---

[1] See Samuel Kaplan, *The Auto Worker in Suburbia, A Replication of Working-Class Suburb*, M.A. thesis, University of California, Berkeley, Department of Sociology, 1965; Herbert Gans, *The Levittowners* (New York: Pantheon Books, 1967); S.D. Clark, *The Suburban Society* (Toronto: University of Toronto Press, 1966); William Dobriner, *Class in Suburbia* (Englewood Cliffs, N.J.: Prentice-Hall, 1963). See also Scott Greer and Shigeo Nohara, "Suburb or Shacktown, the Portrait of an All Negro Community," John Liell, "Social Relationships in a Changing Suburb, A Restudy of Levittown," and Joseph Zelan, "Intellectual Attitudes and Suburban Residence," papers delivered at the 1963 meetings of the American Sociological Association. See also Benjamin Walter and Fred Wirt, "Political Competition in American Suburbs," delivered at the 1966 meetings of the A.S.A. It might be noted here that although the subtitle of the work by John Seeley, *et al.*, is *A Study of the Culture of Suburban Life*, the housing development examined is not actually a "suburb," as that term is used in this book. It is located well within the city of Toronto itself.

dispositions that led them to move to suburbs in the first place; that the variety of physical and demographic differences between cities and suburbs (and there *are* some) bears little significance for the way of life of their inhabitants, and that some of these differences, although statistically accurate, are sociologically spurious, since the appropriate comparisons are not between residential suburbs and cities as wholes, but between suburbs and urban residential neighborhoods. The high degree of order that was asserted as characteristic of suburbia was a result of highly ordered suburbs having been selected for study, and in general the reported changes in the lives of suburbanites were not *caused* by the move to suburbia, but were reasons for moving there in the first place.

In suburbs, as in city apartments, the degree of sociability is determined not primarily by ecological location but by the homogeneity of the population (although as Whyte indicated, the particular flow patterns of sociability may be affected by the specific locations of domiciles). Social class, the age-composition of residents, the age of the neighborhood are much more profound predictors of style of life than is residential location with respect to city limits. Transient attitudes (if they were there to begin with) apparently decline with the increasing age of the suburb, as the neighborhood settles into the style of life determined largely by its dominant social and demographic characteristics, a settling simplified by the economic homogeneity of specific suburban housing tracts. Analysis of national samples has provided confirmation neither of a Republican trend in politics nor a return to religion.

It seems, then, that there are no grounds for believing that suburbia has created a distinctive style of life or a new social character for Americans. Yet what I called "the myth of suburbia" persists, as is evident from the fact that "suburbia" is still very serviceable in public discourse as a highly evocative symbol, and is still eminently discussable over the whole range of our cultural media, from comic books to learned journals. One should not be surprised at this, for myths are seldom dispelled by research; they have something considerably more powerful than mere evidence going for them. And though nothing I say here can change this fact (for knowledge is not power), it is important for us to understand the power of the myth and the nature of its appeal to America's image of itself.

In the final chapter of the book, I undertook a functional explanation of the myth of suburbia: suburbs were rich with visible symbols readily organizable into an image of a way of life which could be marketed to the non-suburban public. The marketing was facilitated by the fact that the myth of suburbia conveniently suited the ideological purposes of several influential groups skilled in the marketing of a variety of social and political opinion. The *descriptive* accuracy of the myth of suburbia went largely unchallenged because it suited the *prescriptive* desires of opinion groups ranging from the yea sayers of the right through the agonizers of the center to the nay sayers of the left.

But though I think this analysis still makes good sense, I think too that there is something more, which I was only dimly aware of then. "Suburbia," I wrote, "is America in its drip-dry Sunday clothes, standing before the bar of history, fulfilled, waiting for its judgement." I suspect now that when I wrote this I was less interested in understanding the full significance of what I felt to be true than I was in simply turning a fancy phrase. But I think now that the notion that Suburbia *is* America is the most recent of our society's periodic attempts to come to terms with the melting pot problem, a problem that goes straight to the heart of the American ambivalence about cultural pluralism.

America has never really come to terms with the legend of the melting pot. That legend, if I may quote the windy text of its original source, saw America as the place where "Celt and Latin, Slav and Teuton, Greek and Syrian, Black and Yellow, Jew and Gentile, the palm and the pine, the pole and the equator, the crescent and the cross" would together build "the Republic of Man and the Kingdom of God."[2] Despite the hope that a unified American culture might emerge from the seething cauldron, it didn't happen; instead, the formation of ethnically homogeneous communities—ghettoes—helped the immigrants preserve large segments of their cultures, and the tendency to endogamy

---

[2] Israel Zangwill, *The Melting Pot* (New York: The Macmillan Co., 1909).

helped them preserve it beyond the first generation. But in spite of the evident facts of our cultural pluralism (by which I mean the persisting correlation of significant differences in values and behavior with ethnic, regional, and social class differences), attempts are continually made to create an image of *the* typical or representative or genuine American and his community, attempts which have usually succeeded only in creating stereotypes—most familiarly, perhaps, a caricature of one or another variety of Our Town: white, Anglo-Saxon, Protestant, and middle class. *Saturday Evening Post* covers, white picket fences, colonial houses, maple hutches, and such have historically played an important role in such attempts. *The myth of suburbia is the latest attempt to render America in this homogeneous manner, to see in the highly visible and proliferating suburban developments a new melting pot which would receive the diverse elements of a new generation from a society fragmented by class, region, religion, and ethnicity, and from them create the American style of life.* Suburbia as America is no falser a picture, probably, than Babbitt or Our Town as America but it fails as a melting pot for the same reason that the original melting pot idea failed: like many other urban neighborhoods, specific suburbs developed a tendency to homogeneity, almost always in terms of social class and very often in terms of ethnicity.

The myth of American cultural homogeneity and the facts of heterogeneity reflect a persistent ambivalence in American society regarding cultural unity and diversity, between the melting pot idea and the pluralist idea. During and after the period of rapid immigration into the "teeming cities," for example, free public education expressed the need for some minimum "Americanization" whereas the ghetto expressed the impulse to cultural self-preservation (both by the natives who excluded and the immigrants who segregated themselves). Fourth of July style patriotic rhetoric expressed the gropings toward an elementary national identity whereas provincial arrogance, and hostility to "the government" and to centers of cosmopolitan influence expressed the affirmation of narrow local autonomies. The ambivalence was really a double ambivalence; each polar position was itself unstable: to be truly tenable, a pluralist ideology must accord intrinsic honor and value to a diversity of life styles, and this it has never completely done; the salient features of minority subcultural styles have more often than not been regarded as stigmata by dominant groups, tolerable so long as they were temporary, that is, *transitional* to something approaching the dominant cultural style. On the other hand, the attempts of provincial, nativist, ("WASP") groups to secure their own style as *the* American style stopped short of supporting the emergence of broadly inclusive *national* institutions which would have facilitated that transition. The most enthusiastic celebrators of "Americanism" were precisely the groups who were most wary of integrating the varieties of the national life into a unified culture.

Indeed, a unified national culture has until quite recently been a most improbable prospect since the United States has traditionally been a society without very powerful national institutions to promote that unity and pass it down the generations. Without an established church or a powerful federal government, without national political parties or a standardized educational system, enormous distances and poor communications enabled local economies to breed a highly differentiated system of *native* subcultures—in addition to those created by the immigrants. Even today, there are probably dozens of distinctive American types, to some extent stereotypes, perhaps, but which nevertheless call attention to the wide variety of *native* styles: Vermont farmers and Boston Brahmins, Southern Bourbons and Tennessee hillbillies, Beatniks and organization men, Plainvillers, Middletowners, and cosmopolitan intellectuals, to say nothing of teenagers, the jet set, and many, many more, all American, all different, and none probably very eager to be integrated into a conceptualization of "American" at a level of complexity suitable for a *Time* cover story or a patriotic war movie.

It is not surprising, then, that when one tries to abstract from American life a system of values which can be called distinctively or representatively American, the task is immensely difficult. The most systematic attempt by a sociologist, that of Robin Williams in his book *American Society*,[3] is foiled by the fact that

---

[3] Robin Williams, *American Society* (New York: Alfred A. Knopf, 1961); see chap. xi.

important groups in American society do not share the 15 or 16 values which he offers as basically American. There is no question that values such as "achievement," "work," "efficiency," "equality," and the rest have played an important part in creating the quality of American life, but important parts of the lower and working classes (important because of their numbers) do not share them, and important parts of the upper class (important because of their influence) do not share them. The very poor are different from you and me, and (as Scott Fitzgerald is said to have remarked to Ernest Hemingway) so are the very rich.

The persistence of the myth of suburbia, then, reveals a continuing tension in American society between the ideals of cultural diversity, and the persistent attempts to find some transcendent principles or values which define the unity of American culture have been compromised by the persistence of important class and ethnic differences. Even under natural or "organic" conditions "American" patterns of culture are enormously difficult to describe with salutary accuracy. This difficulty is exacerbated when a society becomes sophisticated enough to be self-conscious about its culture and rich enough to do something about it. The maturity and the luxury of our civilization constrain its elites to define an "American" style, and the miracle of our technology arms us to manufacture it. Our society is wealthy enough to support a substantial class of intellectuals devoted to staying on top of contemporary events to "spot the trend," "see the pattern," "find the meaning," or "discover the style." And our media are such that these spottings and seeings are more or less instantaneously communicated to audiences of millions, whose demand upon the marketers of opinions and interpretations for sensible and coherent syntheses is greater than the available supply.

Under such conditions, we do not get serious historical interpretation of contemporary events; we do not even get responsible journalism; we get myths, which themselves become part of the forces shaping what is happening, and which hence function ideologically. The myth of suburbia fosters an image of a homogeneous and classless America without a trace of ethnicity but fully equipped for happiness by the marvelous productivity of

American industry: the ranch house with the occupied two-car garage, the refrigerator and freezer, the washer and dryer, the garbage disposal and the built-in range and dishwasher, the color TV and the hi-fi stereo. Suburbia: its lawns trim, its driveways clean, its children happy on its curving streets and in its pastel schools. Suburbia, California style, is America.

Most American intellectuals have found this image repugnant, but the bases of their antipathy have never really been made clear. Somehow associated with these physical symbols of suburbia in the minds of most intellectuals are complacency, smugness, conformity, status anxiety, and all the rest of the by-now-familiar and dreary catalogue of suburban culture. But the casual connection between the physical character and the alleged cultural style of suburbia has never been clearly established. It is almost as if American intellectuals felt, consistent with Puritan tradition, that physical comfort necessarily meant intellectual sloth. Perhaps it is because we have been too well trained to believe that there is somehow a direct relationship between the physical structure or the esthetic shape of a residential environment and the sort of values and culture it can possibly engender —so that the esthetic monotony of suburbia could house nothing but a generation of dull, monotonous people, and its cheerful poverty of architectural design could breed nothing but a race of happy robots. The only trouble with this view is that there is little evidence and less logic to support it. Most of the adult suburbanites were *urban* bred, and hence presumably already shaped by the time they became suburbanites. And although it is still a little too early to tell what kind of culture will be produced by the generation bred in the manufactured environment of suburbia, we might remember that most of the critics of suburbia were bred in the manufactured environment of New York and other big cities.

But becoming aware of the myth of suburbia, and pointing to the disparities between it and what we actually know of suburbs we have closely studied, should not be confused with a *defense* of suburbia. Nor should anything I have said about the critics of suburbia be interpreted as a revelation of my personal bias in favor of suburbia. As I suggested earlier, myths are potent enough to survive evidence; they are not disarmed by under-standing. Quite the contrary. Once myths gain currency, once they go, as we say, "into the cultural air," they *become* real, and function frequently as self-fulfilling prophecies. Life copies litera-ture; fact is affected by fiction; history is constrained by myth. "If a situation is defined as real," said William I. Thomas, "it is real in its consequences," and I have no doubt that family deci-sions regarding whether to move to the suburbs have been affect-ed (both pro and con) by the myth of suburbia. And despite everything reasonable I have said about suburbs, I *know* that the fact that I unreasonably dislike them has been conditioned, *beyond the possibility of redemption by mere research*, by the fact that the myth of suburbia exists.   *B.B.*

Davis, California
January, 1968

Contents

Chapter I

The Myth of Suburbia

In recent years a myth of suburbia has developed in the United States. In saying this, I refer not to the physical facts of the movement to the suburbs; this is an ecological tendency to which all recent statistics on population mobility bear eloquent testimony.[1] I refer instead to the social and cultural ramifications that are perceived to have been inherent in the suburban exodus. Brunner and Hallenbeck, for example, call the rise of suburbia "one of the major social changes of the twentieth century," [2] and the popular literature especially is full of characterizations of suburbia as "a new way of life."

The significance of the past decade cannot be overestimated since it is only in this period that suburbia has become a *mass* phenomenon and hence prone to the manufacture of modern myth. Suburbanization, however, goes back as far as the latter part

---

[1] In 1953, for example, *Fortune* reported that suburban population had increased by 75 per cent over 1934, although total population was increasing by only 25 per cent; between 1947 and 1953 the increase was 43 per cent. See "The New Suburban Market," *Fortune* (November, 1953), p. 234. That this trend is continuing is indicated by a recent Census Bureau report showing that between 1950 and 1956 the population of suburbs increased by 29.3 per cent, although their central cities gained by only 4.7 per cent. For a full discussion of this whole tendency, see Donald Bogue, *Population Growth in Standard Metropolitan Areas, 1900-1950*, especially pp. 18-19, tables 13 and 14, p. 30, and table 19, p. 34.

[2] Edmund deS. Brunner and Wilbur C. Hallenbeck, *American Society: Urban and Rural Patterns*, p. 253.

of the nineteenth century, when the very wealthy began to build country estates along the way of suburban railroad stations. Improvements in the automobile and the development of good highways after World War I brought greater numbers of wealthy people to suburban areas in the 1920's. The depression of the 1930's slowed the process of suburbanization, but the late 1930's saw the development of some new residential construction at the peripheries of city limits. The big boom in suburban development, of course, came after World War II with the proliferation of "the mass produced suburbs" all over the country, and well within the reach of middle- and lower-middle-income people. And in the last few years, suburbanization of secondary and tertiary industry has followed closely upon residential suburbanization. Carl Bridenbaugh has noted that suburbanization began as far back as the early part of the eighteenth century. "One ordinarily thinks of the suburban movement of the present century as being of recent origin, and it will come as a surprise to many that the flight from the city began in the first half of the eighteenth century— and for the same reasons as today. The differences were in degree only. Just as Londoners moved westward from the City in search of quiet, air, comfort, lower rents, and more room for display, so did Philadelphians cross the northern and southern bounds of the metropolis in a perennial search for the 'green.' . . . That greatest of townsmen, Benjamin Franklin, even moved from High Street to Second and Sassafras, grumbling that 'the din of the Market increases upon me; and that, with frequent interruptions, has, I find, made me say some things twice over.' "[3]

The literature on suburbanization seems to fall roughly into two categories. Studies of suburbanization by sociologists have been going on for a long time; with few exceptions, however, these have been primarily ecological or demographic in character.[4] On

[3] See Frederick Lewis Allen's classification of the five stages of suburbanization in "The Big Change in Suburbia, Part I." For some pungent commentaries on the early periods of Suburbanization in this century, see H. A. Bridgman, "The Suburbanite"; Lewis Mumford, "The Wilderness of Suburbia"; H. I. Phillips, "The 7:58 Loses a Passenger"; Christine Frederick, "Is Suburban Living a Delusion?" and Ethel Swift, "In Defense of Suburbia." For the beginnings of suburbanization, see Carl Bridenbaugh, *Cities in Revolt: Urban Life in America, 1743-1776*, p. 24.

[4] Some of the more recent work includes: J. Allen Beegle, "Characteristics of Michigan's Fringe Population"; Noel P. Gist, "Developing Patterns of Urban

the other hand, studies of and comment on the culture and social psychology of suburban life have, again with a few exceptions, been left largely to popular writers, journalists, and intellectuals.[5] To urban sociologists in general, "suburbs" is a term of ecological reference; ecologists and demographers may often dispute the most useful way of conceiving "suburbs" for the purposes of their work, but the dispute is largely a technical one. "Suburbia," on the other hand, is a term of cultural reference; it is intended to connote a way of life, or, rather, the intent of those who use it is to connote a way of life.[6] The ubiquity of the term suburbia in current popular literature suggests that its meaning is well on its way to standardization—that what it is supposed to connote is widely enough accepted to permit free use of the term with a reasonable amount of certainty that it will convey the images it intends. In the last ten or twelve years, these images have coalesced into a full-blown myth, complete with its articles of faith,

---

Decentralization"; Chauncey Harris, "Suburbs"; Lewis W. Jones, "The Hinterland Reconsidered"; Leo F. Schnore, "The Functions of Metropolitan Suburbs"; Leo F. Schnore, "Satellites and Suburbs"; Leo F. Schnore, "The Growth of Metropolitan Suburbs." See also Walter T. Martin, The Rural-Urban Fringe.

[6] See, for example, William H. Whyte's famous series of articles, later revised and reprinted as Part VII of his The Organization Man; Harry Henderson, "The Mass-Produced Suburbs, Part I," and "The Mass-Produced Suburbs, Part II: Rugged American Collectivism"; Frederick Lewis Allen, "The Big Change in Suburbia, Part I," and "The Big Change in Suburbia, Part II: Crisis in the Suburbs"; John Keats, The Crack in the Picture Window; Carl von Rhode, "The Suburban Mind"; William Newman, "Americans in Subtopia," and Maurice Stein, "Suburbia, A Walk on the Mild Side"; and Phyllis McGinley, "Suburbia, Of Thee I Sing." Some of the exceptions, that is, work by sociologists, include John Seeley, et al.; Crestwood Heights . . . ; Sylvia Fava, "Suburbanism as a Way of Life"; David Riesman, "The Suburban Dislocation"; Nathan Whetten, "Suburbanization as a Field for Sociological Research"; Ritchie Lowry, "Toward a Sociology of Suburbia"; and the early works by Harlan P. Douglass, The Suburban Trend, and George Lundberg, et al., Leisure: A Suburban Study; William Dobriner (ed.), The Suburban Community. The following references were published too late for consideration here: Andrew M. Greeley, The Church and the Suburbs, New York, 1959; Albert I. Gordon, Jews in Suburbia, Boston, 1959; Robert C. Wood, Suburbia, Its People and Their Politics, Boston, 1959; Thomas Ktsanes and Leonard Reissman, "Suburbia-New Homes for Old Values," Social Problems, Winter, 1959-1960.

[6] David Riesman comments in a melancholy vein that the ecological work on suburbs and the sociopsychological work do not complement each other: ". . . the characteristic situation in sociology today [is] that research in the macrocosmic and in the microcosmic scarcely connect, scarcely inform each other." David Riesman, op. cit., p. 125.

its sacred symbols, its rituals, its promise for the future, and its resolution of ultimate questions. The details of the myth are rife in many of the mass circulation magazines as well as in more intellectual periodicals and books; and although the details should be familiar to almost everyone interested in contemporary cultural trends, it may be well to summarize them briefly.

ELEMENTS OF THE MYTH

Approaching the myth of suburbia from the outside, one is immediately struck by rows of new ranch-type houses either identical in design or with minor variations in a basic plan, winding streets, neat lawns, two-car garages, infant trees, and bicycles and tricycles lining the sidewalks.[7] Near at hand is the modern ranch-type school and the even more modern shopping center, dominated by the giant supermarket, which is flanked by a pastel-dotted expanse of parking lot. Beneath the television antenna and behind the modestly but charmingly landscaped entrance to the tract home reside the suburbanite and his family. I should perhaps say "temporarily reside" because the most prominent element of the myth is that residence in a tract suburb is temporary; suburbia is a "transient center" because its breadwinners are upward mobile, and live there only until a promotion and/or a company transfer permits or requires something somewhat more opulent in the way of a home. The suburbanites are upward mobile because they are predominantly young (most commentators seem to agree that almost all are between twenty-five and thirty-five), well educated, and have a promising place in some organizational hierarchy—promising because of a continuing expansion of the economy with no serious slowdown in sight. They are engineers, middle-management men, young lawyers, salesmen,

---

[7] The following characterization is a distillation of the literature cited in footnote 5, above. Since what follows is essentially a sketch, the literature, in general, will not be cited. Detailed and specific references to this literature *will* be made, however, in appropriate places in succeeding chapters. In a sense, what follows is more than a sketch; it is really a *definition* of "suburbia," for though there is no standard definition of "suburb" in any rigorous sense (see Brunner and Hallenbeck, *op. cit.*, p. 255), "suburbia" almost universally implies a *tract housing development* within commuting distance of a large city. We will use the terms "suburb" to refer to tract housing developments within standard metropolitan areas and "suburbia" to refer to the kind of life that is said to be led in them. We suggest, however, that commuting is an irrelevant aspect of the definition.

insurance agents, teachers, civil service bureaucrats—occupational groups sometimes designated as organization men, and sometimes as "the new middle class." Most such occupations require some college education, so it comes as no surprise to hear and read that the suburbanites are well educated. Their wives too seem to be well educated; their reported conversation, their patois, and especially their apparently avid interest in theories of child development all suggest their exposure to higher education. According to the myth, a new kind of hyperactive social life has apparently developed in suburbia. This is manifest not only in the informal visiting or "neighboring" that is said to be rife, but also in the lively organizational life that goes on. Associations, clubs, and organizations are said to exist for almost every conceivable hobby, interest, or preoccupation. The hyperactive participation of suburbanites is said to extend beyond the limits of voluntary associations to include an equally active participation in local civic affairs. This active, busy participation by young families is encouraged by the absence of an older generation who, in other communities, would normally be the leaders. The absence of an older generation is said to have an especially strong effect upon the young women of the community who, thrown back upon their own resources, develop a marked independence and initiative in civic affairs. The informal social life revolves around the daytime female "kaffeeklatsch" at which "the girls" discuss everything from the problems of handling salesmen to the problems of handling Susie. In the evening the sociability (made possible by the baby-sitting pool) is continued with rounds of couples dropping in on each other for bridge, a drink, or some conversation.

This rich social life is fostered by the homogeneity of the suburbanites; they are in the same age range and have similar jobs and incomes, their children are around the same age, their problems of housing and furnishing are similar. In short, they have a maximum of similar interests and preoccupations which promote their solidarity. This very solidarity and homogeneity (when combined with the uniformities of the physical context) are often perceived as the sources of "conformity" in the suburbia; aloofness or detachment is frowned upon. The intenseness of the social life is sometimes interpreted as a lack of privacy, and this lack of privacy, when added to the immediate visibility of deviations from accepted norms, permits strong, if informal, sanctions to be wielded against nonconformity. The "involvement of everyone in everyone else's life" submits one to the constant scrutiny of the community, and everything from an unclipped lawn to an unclipped head of hair may be cause for invidious comment. On the other hand, the uniformity and homogeneity make suburbia classless or one-class (variously designated as middle or upper middle class). For those interlopers who arrive in the suburbs bearing the unmistakable marks of a more deprived upbringing, suburbia is said to serve as a kind of "second melting pot" in which those who are mobile upward out of the lower orders learn to take on the appropriate folkways of the milieu to which they aspire.

During the daylight hours, suburbia, in the imagery of the myth, is a place almost wholly given over to child rearing. Manless during the day, suburbia is a female society in which the young mothers, well educated and without the interference of tradition (represented by doting grandparents), can rear their children according to the best modern methods. "In the absence of older people, the top authorities on child guidance [in suburbia] are two books: Spock's *Infant Care,* and Gesell's *The First Five Years of Life.* You hear frequent references to them." [8]

The widely commented upon "return to religion" is said to be most visible in suburbia. Clergymen are swamped, not only with their spiritual duties but with marriage counseling and other family problems as well. The revivified religious life in suburbia is not merely a matter of the increasing size of Sunday congregations; the church is not only a house of worship but a local civic institution also, and as such it benefits from the generally active civic life of the suburbanites.

Part of the myth of suburbia is the image of suburbanites as commuters: they work in the city. For cartoonists and other mythmakers, this mass morning exodus to the city has provided opportunity for the creation of images such as "the race to make the 7:12," getting the station wagon started on a cold morning, or the army of wives waiting at the Scarsdale station for the 5:05 from

---

[8] Harry Henderson, "The Mass-Produced Suburbs, Part II: Rugged American Collectivism," p. 84.

the city. A good deal has been deduced about the way of life in the suburbs from the fact of commuting. For father, commuting means an extra hour or two away from the family, for example, with its debilitating effects upon the relation between father and children. Sometimes this means that Dad leaves for work before the children are up and comes home after they are put to bed. Naturally, these extra hours put a greater burden upon the mother, and have implications for the relation between husband and wife.

In commuting, the commuter returns in the morning to the place where he was bred, for the residents of suburbia are apparently former city people who "escaped" to the suburbs. By moving to the suburbs, however, the erstwhile Democrat from the "urban ward"[9] becomes the suburban Republican. The voting shift has been commented on or worried about at great length; there seems to be something about suburbia that makes Republicans out of people who were Democrats while they lived in the city. But the political life in the suburbs is said to be characterized not only by the voting shift, but by the vigor with which it is carried on. Political activity takes its place beside other civic and organizational activity, intense and spirited.

SOURCES OF THE MYTH

The foregoing characterization is intended neither as ethnography nor as caricature. Brief and sketchy as it is, it does not, I think, misrepresent the typical image of suburbia that, by way of highbrow as well as middlebrow periodicals (as well as some recent books), has come to dominate the minds of most Americans, including intellectuals. It takes scarcely more than a moment's reflection, however, for the perplexing question to arise: why should a group of tract houses, mass produced and quickly thrown up on the outskirts of a large city, apparently generate so uniform a way of life? What is the logic that links tract living with "suburbanism as a way of life"?

If the homes characteristic of suburbia were all within a narrow

---

[9] William Whyte has a way of making the phrase "urban ward" resound with connotations of poverty, deprivation, soot, and brick—as if "urban ward" were a synonym for "slum."

price range, we might expect them to be occupied by families of similar income, and this might account for some of the homogeneity of the neighborhood ethos. But suburban developments are themselves a heterogeneous phenomenon. The term "suburbia" has not only been used to refer to tract-housing developments as low as $7,000 per unit and as high as $65,000 per unit,[10] but also to rental developments whose occupants do not think of themselves as homeowners. The same term has been used to cover old rural towns (such as those in the Westchester-Fairfield county complex around New York City) which, because of the expansion of the city and improvements in transportation, have only gradually become suburban in character;[11] it has been applied also to gradually developing residential neighborhoods near the peripheries of city limits. Clearly, then, the ecological nature of suburbs cannot justify so monolithic an image as that of "suburbia."

If the image of suburbia is limited to the mass-produced tract developments, perhaps it is the fact of commuting that links suburban residence with "suburbanism as a way of life." Clearly, the demands of daily commuting create certain common conditions which might go far to explain some of the ostensible uniformities of suburban living. But certainly commuting is not inherent in suburban living despite the many students of suburbia who have made commuting an essential part of their definitions of suburbs. *Fortune,* for example, says that, "The basic characteristic of suburbia is that it is inhabited by people who work in a city, but prefer to live where there is more open space, and are willing to suffer both inconvenience and expense to live there." Von Rhode says, "The distinguishing aspect of the suburb is, of course, the commuter." And Walter Martin says, ". . . the characteristics essential to suburban status . . . are a unique ecological position in relation to a larger city and a high rate of commuting to that city." These definitions would exclude the community reported

[10] "In a single suburb of Chicago, for example, you can buy ranch houses that cost $10,000 or $65,000 just a few hundred yards apart." Russell Lynes, *The Taste-makers,* p. 253. $7,000 was the original price for homes in Levittown, Long Island.

[11] The articles by Carl von Rhode and Phyllis McGinley, cited earlier, clearly evoke the image of a Connecticut town on Long Island Sound. It is perhaps all to the good that this kind of suburb has recently been designated an "exurb." See A. C. Spectorsky's diverting book, *The Exurbanites.*

on in this study from the category "suburb," but more than t\
ty-five years ago, Lundberg noted, ". . . perhaps too m
has been made of commuting as a phenomenon unique to
suburb. As a matter of fact, comparatively few people in a la
city live within walking distance of their work. From this po
of view a great number of people living in the city are also coi
muters . . . commuting can certainly not be stressed as a uniqu
feature or a fundamental distinction of suburban life as contraste
with urban." [12]

It may have been true that the occupations of most suburbanites required a daily trip to and from the central business district
of the city; it may still be true, but it is likely to be decreasingly
true with the passage of time. The pioneers to the suburban
residential frontier have been followed not only by masses of
retail trade outlets, but by industry also. Modern mass production
technology has made obsolete many two- and three-story plants
in urban areas,[13] and today's modern factories are vast one-story
operations which require wide expanses of land, which are either
unavailable or too expensive in the city itself. Thus with the passage of time, "industrial parks" will increasingly dot suburban
areas, and the proportions of suburbanites commuting to the city
each day will decrease.[14]

If the occupations of most suburbanites were similar in their
demands, this might help account for the development of a gen-
eric way of life in the suburbs. Or indeed, if suburbs were popu-

---

[12] See "The New Suburban Market," p. 129. See also Carl von Rhode, *op. cit.*,
p. 294; Walter T. Martin, "The Structuring of Social Relationships Engendered by
Suburban Residence"; and George Lundberg, *et al.*, *Leisure: A Suburban Study*,
p. 47.

[13] In 1954, *Time* reported, ". . . now industry is seeking the country too, looking for large tracts of open land to build efficient one-story plants. Of 2,658 plants
built in the New York area from 1946 to 1951 only 593 went up in the city
proper." *Time*, "Flight to the Suburbs," (March 22, 1954), p. 102. For more
detailed reports of this trend see Evelyn Kitagawa and Donald Bogue, *Suburbanization of Manufacturing Activities within Standard Metropolitan Areas.* For tertiary
industry, see Raymond Cuzzort, *Suburbanization of Service Industries within Standard Metropolitan Areas,* and James D. Tarver, "Suburbanization of Retail Trade in
the Standard Metropolitan Areas of the U. S., 1948-1954."

[14] What this means, of course, is that increasing numbers of factory workers will
be living in suburbs—not necessarily satellite industrial cities, but new tract suburbs. Woodbury has noted that the decline in the proportion of production workers
in cities has been matched by increases in suburban areas of the same cities. See
Coleman Woodbury, "Suburbanization and Suburbia," p. 7.

lated largely by organization men and their families, then we could understand more readily the style of life that is said to go on. Or, lacking this, if organization men, as Whyte puts it, give the prevailing *tone* to life in the suburbs, then we could more readily understand the prevalence of his model in the literature. But there is no ready hypothesis to explain why the occupations of suburbanites should be so homogeneous. It may be true that the typical organization man is a suburbanite. But it is one thing to assert this and quite another thing to assert that the typical tract suburb is populated by organization men and their families and/or dominated by an "organization" way of life.

Clearly then (and with all due respect for the selective aspects of suburban migration), one suburb is apt to differ from another not only in the price range of its homes, the income characteristics of its residents, their occupational make-up, and the home-to-work traveling patterns of its breadwinners, but also in its educational levels, the character of the region, the size of the suburb, the social-geographical origin of its residents, and countless more indices—all of which, presumably, may be expected to lead to differences in "way of life."

But we not only have good reason to expect suburbs to *differ* markedly from one another; we have reason to expect striking *similarities* between life in urban residential neighborhoods and tract suburbs of a similar socioeconomic make-up. Most residential neighborhoods are "manless" during the day; why not? Husbands are at work, and the only men around are likely to be salesmen and local tradespeople. Even in large cities many men "commute" to work, that is, take subways, buses, or other forms of public transportation to their jobs which may be on the other side of town.[15] Also there are thousands of blocks in American cities with rows of identical or similar houses within a narrow rental or price range, and presumably occupied by families in a similar income bracket.[16] Certainly, urban neighborhoods have always had a class character and a "way of life" associated with them. Certainly the

---

[15] Webster still prefers to define "commuter" as someone who travels by way of a commutation ticket.

[16] The same fears for massification and conformity were felt regarding these urban neighborhoods as are now felt for the mass-produced suburbs. See Riesman, "The Suburban Dislocation," p. 123.

whole image of "conformity" in suburbia closely parallels the older image of the tyranny of gossip in the American small town. There is, then, apparently no reason to believe, no ready and viable hypotheses to explain why "suburbia" should be the new and homogeneous phenomenon it is usually conceived to be. What are the sources of the alleged new way of life? Why should the occupations of suburbanities be so homogeneous? Why should there be more conformity? Why should the "social life" be so intense? Why should organizational participation be so widespread? Why should the churches be so much busier than elsewhere? Why should educational levels be so much higher than average? Why should the residents vote Republican? In short, why does "suburbia" set off this chain reaction of images, associations, and ideas that have coalesced into a single myth?

WORKING-CLASS SUBURBS

This is, of course, a large question, and it would be premature to attempt an answer at this point. It is enough for the present to observe that the myth of suburbia flourishes in spite of an apparent lack of logic in its formulation. In continually referring to "the myth of suburbia" I do not mean to imply that the reports on the culture of suburban life have been falsified, and it would be a mistake to interpret the tone of my remarks as a debunking one. I mean only to say that the reports we have had so far are extremely selective; they are based, for the most part, upon life in Levittown, New York; Park Forest, Illinois; Lakewood, near Los Angeles; and, most recently (the best study so far), a fashionable suburb of Toronto, Canada. The studies that have given rise to the myth of suburbia have been studies of *middle-class suburbs*, that is, suburbs of very large cities[17] populated primarily by people in the occupational groups often thought of as making up the "new middle class"—the engineers, teachers, and organization men

---

[17] Suburbanization, of course, has not only occurred around our largest cities, but around smaller ones as well: ". . . with the exception of a general tendency for SMA's of one million inhabitants or more to grow at a slightly less rapid rate than SMA's smaller than this, there has been no pronounced or consistent trend for rates of total metropolitan growth to vary with size. . . ." Quoted by Woodbury, *op. cit.*, from Bogue, *op. cit.* David Riesman has observed, "so far as I can see we know almost nothing about the suburbs (old or new) surrounding the smaller cities." David Riesman, *op. cit.*, p. 124.

mentioned earlier.[18] If the phrase "middle-class suburb" strikes the
eye as redundant, it is testimony to the efficacy of the myth, for
as I have suggested, there is certainly no reason to believe that
residence in a new tract suburb in and of itself immediately (or
even within a few years) generates a uniquely new middle-class
style of life. Nor is there any reason to believe that the self-selec-
tive processes of suburban migration are such that suburbs attract
an overwhelming majority of white-collar people to them.

These remarks are intended to suggest that the extant image
of suburbia may be a distorted one; that its accuracy may be
limited to the suburbs of great metropolises which are populated
by former residents of the central city who work in its white-collar
hierarchies. Thus whereas in most minds, Westchester and Nassau counties in New York, and Park Forest, Illinois, are ideal
typical representatives of "suburbia," they may, in fact, be representative only of suburbs of great cities and of a way of life lived
by metropolis-bred, well-educated people of white-collar status.
If this or something like this is, in fact, the case, then it is clearly
a mistake to identify "suburbanism" exclusively with the kind of
life that is said to go on in places like these. Large tracts of suburban housing, in many respects indistinguishable from those on
Long Island and in Park Forest, have gone up and are continuing
to go up all over the country, not only near large cities, but near
middle-sized and small ones as well. And if, as is not unlikely,
many of the residents of these are rural-bred, with relatively little
education, and innocent of white-collar status or aspirations, then
we may expect sharp differences between their social and cultural
life and that of their more sophisticated counterparts in white-collar suburbs.

This is hardly a revolutionary supposition; indeed, the fact

---

[18] The Toronto study is frankly a study of a wealthy suburb and is, without
doubt, quite reliable. The unanimity about well-studied Park Forest also lends
credence to its portrayal. However, Levittown, New York, and Lakewood, California, are more ambiguous cases. One sharp resident of Levittown writes me
that suburb is not *only* white collar, but contains plenty of "blue collar, frayed
collar, and turned collar people also," and that the different groups have different
ways of life. The vast Lakewood development is heavily populated with southern
California aircraft workers, and there is considerable doubt that *Newsweek's*
report on Lakewood, so heavily laden with the mobility motif, took adequate
account of them.

that it should have to be asserted at all is still further testimony
to the vitality of the myth I have been describing. This study,
then, is based upon the most conventional of sociological assump-
tions: that a "way of life" is a function of such variables as age, income, occupation, education, rural-urban background, and so
forth, and that this is as true for suburbs as it is for any other kind
of modern comunity. To be more specific, a mass-produced tract
suburb, rapidly occupied, has little chance to develop gradually a
neighborhood "character" of its own. It is thus quite likely that a
mass-produced suburb of, say, Chicago or New York, which at-
tracts a large group of relatively well-educated, white-collar New
Yorkers or Chicagoans, is apt to take on the "social character" (in
Fromm's phrase) which was incipient while the young suburbanites were still resident in the urban apartments of their parents;
the "other directedness" they learned in the city may, in the physical context of the tract suburb, be permitted its full development.
On the other hand, as I have repeatedly emphasized, there is no
reason to suppose that most suburbs have this character of sophisticated "urbanism transplanted." There *is* good reason to suppose
that increasing numbers of unquestionably working-class people
will be migrating to new tract suburbs; *not,* it should be emphasized, to new suburbs immediately and visibly characterizable as
"working class," but to suburbs which to all intents and purposes
look from the *outside* like the fulfillment of the promise of America
symbolized in the myth. Large numbers of semiskilled as well as
skilled factory workers in strongly unionized heavy industry are
clearly able to afford to buy new tract homes in the $12,000 to
$16,000 price range;[19] many are doing so, and presumably even
more will be doing so as increasing numbers of factories move out
of the city to the hinterlands. This study is a report of research
carried on in such a suburb.

   In his Introduction to Eli Chinoy's *Automobile Workers and
the American Dream,* David Riesman wonders "what will happen
to the worker when he has his 'nice little modern home.'" [20] Riesman's question was prompted by Chinoy's report that automobile

---

[19] *Time* reports that 27 per cent of all new American homes fall into the price
category represented by the $13,000 house shown at the U. S. exhibition in Moscow
in the summer of 1959. *Time,* April 20, 1959, p. 91.
   [20] Eli Chinoy, *Automobile Workers and the American Dream,* p. xx.

workers identified getting ahead with achieving "a nice little modern house of my own." The present study may be viewed as a partial response to Riesman's curiosity. It has, however, a double focus: it is not only a study of a suburb, it is also a study of working-class life; as such, it is a twin to Chinoy's book. Both his work and this deal with automobile workers and the American dream. Chinoy's focus was the factory; mine is the suburb.

Chapter II

The Question of Mobility

Perhaps the most prominent feature of suburbia, as it has been characterized in the popular literature, is its transient nature. The logic of William H. Whyte's inclusion of his chapters on suburbia in *The Organization Man* is that suburbia represents the organization man *at home*, that is to say, temporarily at home, because organization men are the archetypal "transients"—a word which Whyte saw fit to use both as a chapter title and as a concept which binds much of his book together. But the notion of "suburbia" as a transient center and of suburbanites as socially mobile men is not at all unique with Whyte; we find it rife in virtually all of the popular literature in the field. In its big spread on suburbia, *Newsweek* characterized Lakewood (Los Angeles County) as such a transient community.[1] Using Levittown, New York, as his model, Harry Henderson characterizes that new tract suburb similarly: "What sets them [the suburbanites] apart from social groups in older American communities is their lack of rigid definition of 'who belongs.' This is primarily a result of their transience, the fact that they expect to move, both physically and in terms of

---

[1] ". . . Suburbia is also a hotbed of yet another U. S. custom: 'Upgrading,' the continuing movement toward bigger houses, better neighborhoods, and more possessions as incomes rise and more children arrive." *Newsweek* (April 1, 1957), p. 36.

income." [2] For Andrew Greeley, "upward mobility is the suburbanite's public mania. As he climbs the success ladder, he also swaps the old neighborhood for the new." [3] Father Greeley's account of the stages of suburban upward mobility is considerably more sanguine than John Keats' rather less than elegiac account of the dreary road by which the tract house purchaser treads "upward." [4] Russell Lynes says that "The quality of these mass-produced communities that distinguishes them from the suburbs of the twenties and thirties is that their populations are highly mobile and that they are almost entirely inhabited by families in the same age and income group." [5] Even in *Dissent*, a periodical not notable for its celebration of the American way of life, we find a characterization of suburbia as "the institutionalization of mobility." [6]

In the suburb reported on here, however, very little, if any, socially mobile attitudes are in evidence. [7] Of the total sample, 94 per cent reported that they thought of their jobs with Ford as "permanent" jobs; only 3 per cent were keeping their eyes open for something better. It should be remembered that these respondents are almost [8] all hourly wage workers with relatively poor educations, and their apparent intent to stay with Ford does not indicate any real hope of rising in the company hierarchy. "If I found something better, I'd take it," said one respondent, "but you can bet that this job is permanent." Another respondent, who

---

[2] Harry Henderson, "Rugged American Collectivism: The Mass-Produced Suburbs, Part II," p. 80.

[3] Andrew M. Greeley, "Suburbia, A New Way of Life," p. 13.

[4] John Keats, *The Crack in the Picture Window*.

[5] Russell Lynes, *The Tastemakers*, p. 252.

[6] See William Newman, "Americans in Subtopia," and Maurice Stein, "Suburbia —A Walk on the Mild Side." Both articles are really review articles of John Seeley, *et al.*, *Crestwood Heights*, a study of a wealthy suburb of Toronto, Canada. Both Newman and Stein, however, do not hesitate to generalize from Crestwood Heights to "suburbia" wherever it may be found.

[7] I should emphasize that in saying this I do not suggest that this result invalidates other results. I mean only to reassert this: that "suburb"—even "new tract suburb"—are not synonyms for "middle-class suburb," and that upward mobility is not a special characteristic of suburban residence. To be sure, many upward mobile people live in suburbs; just as surely, many are able to find a way of life congenial to both their aspirations and their achievements in the city.

[8] The sample turned up one individual who had recently quit his job with Ford and opened a service station at a main intersection of the tract, and another individual who had just been promoted from foreman to the salaried position of engineer. Both were less than 35 and were high school graduates.

thought that his chances of getting ahead were "fair," added, "just as good as with any other large concern; they're not going to fold up tomorrow." These remarks seem to be as much a statement of one's lack of comparative prospects as they are estimates of one's chances of getting ahead. At the same time, they may also be interpreted as evidence of a sense of some achievement. To be "just as well off" as one would be with any other company may express either or both a feeling of being trapped and a feeling of having approached the limits of one's potentialities. These two feelings are not irreconcilable.

As appendix table A.1 shows, 43 per cent of the total sample freely admitted that they harbored little or no hope of getting ahead. Nevertheless, 40 per cent felt that their chances of getting ahead in the company were "fair," and 17 per cent were confident enough to say that they felt their chances were "good." Adding these last two figures together, we could conclude that 57 per cent of the Ford workers feel that they have a fair or better chance of getting ahead; but there is good reason to believe that many of this 57 per cent were responding to the question ideologically or stereotypically rather than in terms of a realistic estimate of their actual chances. With their limited educations, there is not much possibility of their rising to managerial or salaried status;[9] foreman is as far as they can reasonably expect to go, yet (excluding those who are already foremen) 64 per cent of the sample reported that they did not *want* to be foremen.[10] Although 32 per cent said that they *would* like to be foremen, the percentage dropped to 21 when it was asked whether they realistically expected to become foremen. So although 57 per cent expect to "get ahead," only 21 per cent expect to realize that expectation by being promoted to foreman (appendix table A.2).

But besides the inference that many of the responses to this question were stereotyped, there is another inference to be made: realizing that their objective possibilities for any major advance are slight (as many of them do), their criteria of "getting ahead"

---

[9] Still, 11 per cent of the total sample said that they *did* expect to become managers or executives, but of this 11 per cent, foremen and the two cases cited in footnote 8 constituted a substantial majority.

[10] The reason most often cited was that foremen have too many worries: "They have to take too much."

become extremely refined, so that, for example, a shift from an assembly line job to a job as, say, stock checker (with barely any wage differentiation) is perceived by the worker as a promotion, as "getting ahead." [11] This inference is suggested not only by our data but by other studies which report that these minute discriminations exist meaningfully for factory workers with limited opportunities and aspirations.[12] From a functionalist viewpoint we could argue that the development of these minute status discriminations reflect a *need* for some framework of status, for some set of achievement criteria viable for people who have no real possibility of crossing class or status lines—when these lines are conceived at the level of society as a whole. These minute distinctions could be assigned the function of *cushioning* the fact of *relative* immobility (that is, failure, in a society in which manual labor at an hourly wage is marked low in the occupational scale) by sustaining a sense of *mobile identity* in a society in which mobility is promised to all but which only some can actually achieve.

Not surprisingly, in view of the relatively low level of occupational aspiration, the evidence indicates that the suburb in which these workers live is not a markedly transient one. Although 21 per cent of the total sample reported that they expected to move within the foreseeable future, appendix table A.3 shows that 73 per cent think of their new tract homes as "permanent." Only 10 per cent reported that there was a lot of turnover in their blocks, but 57 per cent reported that there was "hardly any." This discrepancy in perception of turnover (i.e., sale and repurchase of homes) may be interesting to students of selective perception because those respondents who themselves expected to move perceived much more turnover in the suburb than those who thought of their homes as "permanent."

What little evidence of mobile orientations or of incipient social mobility appears in this suburb seems to be a function not of suburban residence but of factors present in the suburbanite's

---

[11] A few of the unskilled, non-line workers made this explicit by supporting their statements of expectation by saying that they already *had* gotten ahead, that is, by getting off the assembly line.

[12] See, for example, Eli Chinoy, *Automobile Workers and the American Dream,* pp. 64-65; and Leonard Reissman, "Levels of Aspiration and Social Class," pp. 241-242. See also C. R. Walker and R. H. Guest, *The Man on the Assembly Line.*

background before he ever became a suburbanite. Thus, although
we reported that 94 per cent of the total sample thought of their
jobs with Ford as permanent, 100 per cent of those with an eighth
grade education or less thought of their jobs with Ford as permanent. More revealing (see appendix table A.1) is the fact that of
those with an eighth grade education or less, only 5 per cent
thought their chances of getting ahead were good, whereas 35 per
cent of all those with a high school education or more were
willing to say that their chances of getting ahead were good.
Appendix table A.2 shows further relations between education
and expectations of promotion up the hierarchy; in general, the
higher one's education, the higher one's occupational expectation.

But it is not only the relatively well educated who tend to show
what little mobile orientations there are; the young, the urban
born, and those who have already experienced some promotion
seem strikingly more mobile in their expectations than the older
workers, the rural born, and those without experience of promotion. Thus, although 55 per cent of the 20- to 29-year-old workers
thought of their homes as permanent, 81 per cent of the 40- to
49-year-old workers thought of their homes as permanent.
Whereas 39 per cent of the 20- to 29-year olds had no expectations of becoming foremen, 70 per cent of the 40- to 49-year olds
had no expectations of becoming foremen; of those workers more
than 50, none expected to become foremen. Whereas only 14 per
cent of the 20- to 29-year-old group felt that they did not have
much chance of getting ahead, 65 per cent of the 40- to 49-year-
old group felt that they did not have much chance of advancement; 88 per cent of those older than 50 felt that they did not
have much chance of getting ahead. Sixty-eight per cent of the
20- to 29-year-old group did not expect to become managers or
executives, but 79 per cent of the 30- to 39-year-old group, 97 per
cent of the 40- to 49-year-old group, and 100 per cent of the group
older than 50 did not expect to become managers or executives.
(See appendix tables A.1, A.2, A.3.)

Similar results emerge when mobility variables are broken
down by place of birth. Of the urban born, 24 per cent felt that
their chances of getting ahead were good; 15 per cent of the rural
born and none of the foreign born felt this way. Whereas 24 per

cent of the urban born felt that they did *not* have much chance of getting ahead, 52 per cent of the rural born felt this way. Similarly, 30 per cent of the urban born expect to become foremen; but 16 per cent of the rural born and none of the foreign born expect to become foremen. (See appendix tables A.1 and A.2.)

Breaking the total sample this time by job, we again find similar results. Eighty-four per cent of the semiskilled assembly line workers thought of their homes as permanent; 67 per cent of the skilled workers thought of their homes as permanent, but *only 33 per cent of the foremen* expected to remain in the tract permanently. Only 8 per cent of the semiskilled assembly line workers estimated their chances of getting ahead as "good" and only 15 per cent of the semiskilled non-line workers, but 58 per cent of the foremen saw their chances of getting ahead as "good." [13] The aspirational "shot in the arm" that becoming a foreman implies is suggested by the fact that 42 per cent of the foremen expected to become managers or executives; no more than 6 per cent of any of the other groups of workers expected to become managers or executives. (See appendix tables A.1 and A.2.) All these data support the perfectly conventional conclusion that what little aspirations and mobile orientations are evidenced in this suburb are functions of education, youth, an urban background, and some *experience* of advancement.

What aspirations most of these suburbanites do harbor are reserved primarily for their children, and the possibilities of upward mobility are seen as a function of education. An overwhelming majority of the sample say they want college educations for their sons. These desires, however, are largely utopian because most of the respondents qualified their answers with statements such as "if he wants it" and/or "if I can afford it." Of course, many of their sons will be weaned away from any desires for higher education by the normal processes of working-class socialization, and many parents will without doubt find that they simply cannot afford to finance a four-year college education for their sons.

---

[13] Curiously enough, the skilled workers had consistently lower expectations occupationally than both unskilled groups of workers. This is probably so because the rank of foreman is less clearly seen as an advancement by skilled workers than it is by unskilled workers. The wage difference is small, and to become a foreman means giving up their skilled trade.

(Even in this age of "unparalleled prosperity" many of these suburbanites live somewhat beyond their incomes. Sixty-five per cent of the respondents reported that $100 a week or more take-home pay was necessary to support a family of four adequately; only 40 per cent of the respondents actually take home $100 a week or more.) Other parents will find, by the time their sons are of college age, that they are either unable or unwilling to do without the earning power of their sons for another four years. Since it is very doubtful that many parents will be able to save any money expressly for the purpose of their children's education (if, indeed, they are able to save any money at all), the ones who will go to college will be largely those who are both strongly motivated enough to fend for themselves financially and whose parents are willing not only to do without the earning power of the child for another four years, but also actively to encourage him toward a college career. Some indication of the vagueness and the vicariousness of these parents' hopes for their children is contained in appendix table A.4, which lists the occupational preferences of the parents for their children. None, of course, hoped his children would follow in his occupational footsteps. What is striking is the vagueness of many of the occupations listed; in spite of continued probing, 30 respondents clung to their view that their son's occupational choice was "up to him." Only engineer and doctor outranked professional ball player (2 baseball, 1 football) in the specific occupational preferences of these parents for their sons.

In spite of the fact that the study turned up very little evidence of attitudes that we could properly call "socially mobile," that is, some sort of status anticipation and aspiration, the vast majority of our respondents felt that their lives had been distinctly enriched since they had moved from Richmond. This is hardly surprising, for in a sense we are dealing with a case of residential mobility with occupation, income, and most other variables held constant. The residential change has, in the great majority of the cases, constituted a clear improvement; they not only live in more comfortable and more spacious quarters, but they are generally more satisfied with their lives in the San Jose suburb than they were in Richmond. That their former living arrangements were not very desirable is indicated by the fact that 57 per cent of the sample were glad about the movement of the plant—when they *first heard* of its imminence—indicating an absence of the normal reluctance to pull up one's roots once they have been sunk for some time. This is a reflection of the facts that Richmond has a large Negro population (disturbing to Southerners),[14] a generally drab, industrial façade, and the fact that many of the respondents lived in substandard government housing in a city which was never distinguished for the hospitality it showed to its wartime in-migrants. However, in spite of the substandardness of the government housing, the apartments were nevertheless an astounding bargain at the price. Although the vast majority of its residents were glad to get out, a few were sorry to leave such a good thing. One suburbanite, in the comfort of his living room, reminisced about his ambivalence regarding "the housing": "I'm sure glad the plant forced us to move; if it hadn't, we'd probably still be in housing; it was just too cheap to leave." On the other hand, apparently plenty did leave—with disastrous consequences for productivity at the plant. Although the stated major reason for Ford's move was the obsolescence of the Richmond plant, rumors were rife that the unavailability of permanent housing in the Richmond area at prices Ford workers could afford to pay, was also behind the move. Apparently, permanently housed workers (with a mortgage on their backs) are reliable workers.

Of the 33 per cent who were unhappy about the move when they heard it was imminent, more than half were homeowners, but in the approximately two years and a half between the time of the move and the time of the interviews, the 57 per cent who had been happy about the move in February, 1955, had grown to 86 per cent. At the time of the interviews only 4 per cent were still sorry that they moved.

These figures clearly indicate that an immense majority of the sample feel that they are "better off" in San Jose, that in some way their lives have been strikingly improved as a result of mov-

---

[14] As late as two years after the movement of the plant, large numbers of Negro Ford workers had been unable to find satisfactory housing in the San Jose area, and were consequently commuting each day between Richmond and the plant. There is only one new tract suburb in the area which accepts Negroes; others have found homes in the substantial Negro community across the bay in East Palo Alto.

ing. But it would be a mistake to interpret this feeling in terms of class or status mobility. Although 31 per cent of the sample were homeowners before the movement of the plant, 94 per cent of the sample feel that their new suburban houses are superior to the ones they lived in previously—which indicates that even the homeowners did not own anything really substantial. The achievement of a certain level of domestic comfort seems to be about the extent of any major change in their living style; most of the features of life reportedly characteristic of Levittown, Park Forest, and other suburbs of their kind are notable by their absence.[15]

But if their sense of being "better off" is best *not* interpreted in terms of social mobility, how should it be interpreted? First of all, the Grapes of Wrath image of the working class as holloweyed, mute, unconscious, exploited, and poverty-stricken must be dispensed with. The fact is that within the last fifteen or twenty years, large segments of the organized working class have achieved a standard of living enabling them to live comfortable, self-respecting lives (the fact that another depression would destroy all this, at least for some time, does not vitiate the argument I am making here). The important point, however, is that this achievement is almost wholly a matter of money, and it is a great mistake to equate an income which permits most of the basic amenities of what the middle class calls "decency" with becoming middle class. Social mobility characteristically occurs when an occupational advance or a rise in income permits the mobile family to move out of its social milieu into one more in keeping with its aspirations and its new economic status. In the case under discussion this has not happened. Instead, a whole stratum has collectively raised its standard of living simply by buying new homes in the suburbs. The nature of the stratum itself, however, remains largely unchanged. One might think that the major reason for preferring the suburb would be a sense of *social* arrival, but the reasons most frequently cited were reasons having to do with the *physical* or *natural* desirability of the suburb. For example, "the weather" was the most frequently cited reason for preferring the

---

[15] That is to say, most still carry a lunch pail; they don't belong to organizations; they don't entertain much and don't visit their friends much; there has been no increase in their church attendance generally, and no Republican trend in their voting.

San Jose suburb to Richmond. Also frequently mentioned were things like "more room," or convenience to Santa Cruz ocean resorts, or lack of congestion and crowdedness; relatively rare were status-conscious answers such as "nicer neighbors" or "a finer class of people."

A period of prosperity apparently creates not only increased opportunities for social mobility *between* strata, but also enables the traditionally "downtrodden" strata to arrive at a minimum standard of living at which they cannot reasonably be characterized as "depressed" or "deprived." When this occurs, considerable ambiguity is created for students of stratification who rely on gross objective criteria; high wages, low interest rates, and credit buying with "no down payment" almost literally enable the working class to clothe itself in the symbols traditionally worn by the middle class. Certainly, those of us interested in material progress can applaud such a development, but it does not contribute to our understanding of social stratification to point to the evidence of widespread material well-being and announce that America is now a middle-class society. What seems to be happening is that class and status lines are being revised upward. Since stratification is inherently relative or *comparative*, a period which financially enables almost *everyone* to clothe himself in symbols previously associated only with a class, is also likely to produce a restructuring of the symbolic aspects of stratification in order that *distinctions* may be maintained.[16] There is a *conceptual* problem behind the terminological need to break the "middle class" into an "upper" and a "lower" stratum.

What I am suggesting here is that these suburbanites are not *socially* mobile; although their lives have been bettered as a result of a collective residential shift, they have achieved a standard of living beyond which most of them do not expect to rise, and, perhaps, beyond which they feel they have no further *right* to aspire. It was extraordinary how often my question inquiring about their chances of getting ahead was met with expressions of incredulity

---

[16] That something like this is dimly recognized is indicated by the common belief that the 1958 lag in automobile sales was due to the obsolescence of the automobile as a symbol of status, or at any rate, conventional American automobiles.

that I should even have to *ask*. Comments such as "Naagh, I'm
as far as I'm going to go," and "A working man will never get
ahead," and "You have to have a college education to get any-
where," and the starkly simple "You don't never get ahead, I don't
think," were common. In appraising the amount of turnover in
the tract many were quick to point out "It isn't any of the Ford
workers who are moving" or "The ones who moved out were the
snobs." In short, these homes in the suburb are for most of the
workers the end of the line. The rationale probably goes something like this: "Here I am the son of a sharecropper with a ninth
grade education and no really salable skills, and look at me: I'm
paying off a nice new home, have a good car (often two), my kids
and my wife are decently dressed; she has a washing machine,
I have some power tools; what more do I have a right to expect?"

Of the total sample, 66 per cent evaluated the tract as the very
best kind of neighborhood to live in. Of the former residents of
the government housing in Richmond, 80 per cent evaluated the
tract as the best kind of neighborhood to live in. Even a substantial majority of those who had owned homes before the move
evaluated the tract as a first-rate place to live. Only one out of the
total sample felt that the tract was not at all a good place to live.
This evaluation of the suburb is, of course, not conclusive, but the
evidence does suggest that the suburb represents to them if not
"the fulfillment of the promise of America," then at least the fulfillment of whatever they feel they have a right to expect from
"America."

I suggested earlier that any development of middle-class style
in this suburb will probably take a generation to become apparent,
and that even this prediction might be negatively affected by factors which at this time it is impossible to foresee (such as the
possibility that the suburb may develop into a slum). Whyte's
view is that "They [the new suburbs] have become the second
great melting pot. The organization man furnishes the model, and
even in suburbs where he is a minority, he is influential out of all
proportion to his numbers. As the newcomers to the middle class
enter suburbia, they must discard old values, and their sensitivity
to those of the organization man is almost statistically demonstra-

ble." [17] What is misleading in Whyte's statement is that although he says "newcomers to the middle class" the impact of the passage quoted is to suggest "newcomers to suburbia." The point is that newcomers to the middle class arrive there typically by way of the "new middle-class occupations," and regardless of whether they enter suburbia they would in any case presumably be in the process of discarding the values and culture associated with their humble beginnings (a process often begun in college, while preparing themselves for their middle-class occupations). Newcomers to *suburbia,* however, are not at all necessarily fated to be cast in the die of the organization man. Whyte himself recognizes this in his brief discussion of "Eastgate," a tract adjacent to Park Forest, but which, from his brief description of it, is clearly working class in character; but ". . . both the Eastgaters and the others in the community sense that Eastgate is not quite a part of Park Forest. Many Eastgaters have moved to another sector at the first opportunity, and it will probably always remain a bit of alien soil in the one-class society." [18] With these few words, Whyte apparently votes Eastgate out of suburbia, and fails to see that if indeed *suburbia* is the melting pot, it is precisely in Eastgate that he should have looked for the simmering evidence. For *not* to find it in Eastgate and *still* to assert that suburbia is a melting pot constitutes not an empirical observation, but a tautology: suburbs which are not melting pots are not suburbs; that is, suburbs are melting pots by definition.

If the suburb under discussion here contained an influential minority of middle-class people, then we might expect some middle-class resocialization to occur among its factory worker residents. But it is a heavily working-class community; "no executives around here," said one respondent, and he was not far off the mark. A check on the two closest neighbors of the respondents revealed that 69.5 per cent of them are factory workers and most of the remainder are in lower white-collar occupations such as bank teller, postman, policeman, and so forth. In short, the new neighbors of our respondents are for the most part the same kind

---

[17] William H. Whyte, Jr., *The Organization Man,* p. 331.
[18] *Ibid.,* p. 340.

of neighbors they had in Richmond;[19] the milieu remains largely unchanged. That those families who *have* moved out of the tract were characterized as "snobs" and that those Ford workers who expect to move out of the tract within the foreseeable future are primarily foremen and skilled workers indicate that those who aspire to middle-class style and have some slim chance of achieving it are not finding the suburb very satisfactory. But these are relatively few, and what we are *primarily* dealing with here is not an instance of social mobility but instead, the movement of a whole stratum to a new level of domestic comfort. But because the neighborhood is composed predominantly of working-class people, they have not, by moving into the suburb, moved into a new cultural milieu.[20]

---

[19] It did not occur to me until the interviewing was well under way that a distinction I had made between "neighbors" and "friends from the plant" was entirely inappropriate because their neighbors *are,* to a considerable extent, fellow Ford workers.

[20] That they have not will be demonstrated in the chapters to follow. It seemed to me curiously revealing of working-class mentality that, although 12 per cent reported some white-collar experience, many more thought of their military experience as white collar. Some of those with stock jobs in the plant thought of these as white-collar jobs.

Chapter III

Republicans or Democrats?
Politics in a Working-Class Suburb

In the spring of 1957, *Newsweek* was only repeating what seemed to be a well-worn truth when it noted that: "When a city dweller packs up and moves his family to the suburbs, he usually acquires a mortgage, a power lawn mower, and a backyard grill. Often, although a lifelong Democrat, he also starts voting Republican." [1] Apparently this trend was first seriously noticed after the 1952 election, when, of the 67 counties included by the Census Bureau in its classification of the 20 largest metropolitan regions in the United States, 51 went Republican. [2] It is true that, before World War II, most suburban areas outside of the South were normally Republican, but in recent years "even in suburban areas traditionally Democratic, there has been evidence of a tendency toward Republicanism." [3] With the hindsight of two weeks after the 1952 election, *Time* noted retrospectively that the transplantation of hundreds of thousands of city dwellers—many of them Democrats—had raised the question of which way "the suburban

---

[1] *Newsweek* (April 1, 1957), p. 42. Cf. Stanley Rowland's statement of the same genre: ". . . one moves there [to suburbia], buys the right car, keeps his lawn like his neighbor's, eats crunchy breakfast cereal, and votes Republican." "Suburbia Buys Religion," p. 82.

[2] See Edward Janosik, "The New Suburbia."

[3] *Ibid.*

vote" would go. With satisfaction, *Time* reported that the new suburbs "turned in big Republican leads from New York's bedroom counties all across the U. S. . . . Said Chicago's Democratic Boss Jack Arvey (after the Democrats had lost his Cook County): 'The suburbs were murder.' " [4] The suburban tendency to vote Republican was recorded also by Harry Henderson, who, after a survey of some suburban communities, reported, "Politically, the people in these communities have steadily voted Republican . . . in some communities chapters of the Americans for Democratic Action are active, but in no community were they an important force." [5] William H. Whyte has noted the same trend:

Figures rather clearly show that people from big urban Democratic wards tend to become more Republican and, if anything, more conservative than those whose outlook they are unconsciously adopting. . . .

Whatever the cause, it is true that something does seem to happen to Democrats when they get to suburbia. Despite the constant influx of Democrats the size of the Republican vote remains fairly constant from suburb to suburb. [6]

Whatever it is that happens to urban Democrats when they become suburbanites, there is some evidence to suggest that it is not happening uniformly; the size of the Republican vote is not fairly constant from suburb to suburb. Although the tremendous influx of urban New Yorkers into Levittown, Long Island, apparently did little to disrupt the domination of J. Russel Sprague's Republican organization in Nassau County (Long Island), the development of Levittown, Pennsylvania, with its large population of steel workers, resulted in continually decreasing Republican pluralities in Bucks County, Pennsylvania (which previously had been overwhelmingly Republican in character), and finally in local Democratic victories in 1955. [7] Even here, however, the evidence is not uniform. A recent student of Levittown, Long Island, has written, "Irish Catholics in Levittown are switching alle-

---

[4] *Time* (November 17, 1952), p. 24.

[5] Harry Henderson, "Rugged American Collectivism: The Mass Produced Suburbs, Part II," p. 85.

[6] William H. Whyte, Jr., *The Organization Man*, pp. 331-332.

[7] In 1954 the Republican candidate for governor of Pennsylvania took Bucks County by a little more than 1,000 votes. In 1955 the Democrats elected seven out of ten candidates in local elections. See Janosik, *op. cit.*, p. 93.

giances from Democrats to Republicans, but this is happening to Irish Catholics throughout the nation. Jewish voters who have been traditionally Democratic in their voting habits continue to vote Democratic in Levittown." [8] On the other hand, Harry Gersh reports of a New York suburb that, "The forecasters spoke so knowingly of the increase in Democratic votes because of the influx of urban voters into Suburbia. But a 100 per cent increase in the Jewish vote in our area somehow didn't budge the rock-hard Republican majority. The Jewish voter . . . found he wasn't a bloc. . . . So many turned so easily into Republicans. . . ." [9]

Samuel Lubell is one of the few students who have challenged the now widespread assumption that urban Democrats can be expected to start voting Republican as soon as they become suburbanites:

. . . one might expect people to turn Republican as they mount to better income heights. . . . But in large part as the poor and under-privileged prospered . . . they remained loyal to the Democratic party. . . . In Arlington, a fairly well-to-do suburb outside of Boston, I asked one middle-aged man why he hadn't turned Republican when he moved into suburban surroundings. He replied, "I own a nice home, have a new car and am much better off than my parents were. I've been a Democrat all my life. Why should I change?" [10]

The question is reasonable, and those students of suburbia who have been most struck by the Republican trend shown by the voting figures have been hard pressed to find an answer. Among the answers most frequently cited are (1) owning a house and land sensitizes one to taxes, and is in general a conservative influence, and (2) local Republican organization is entrenched in sub-urban areas, and because their organization is strong, party work-ers can be very effective in winning new adherents to the party among the new suburbanites. More recently it has been argued that anxiety to conform to a milieu previously Republican in

---

[8] Harold L. Wattel, "Levittown: A Suburban Community," in William Dobriner (ed.), *The Suburban Community*, p. 299.

[9] See Gersh, "The New Suburbanites of the 50's," p. 217. Contrast Wattel's findings regarding the political behavior of Jews with the remarks of Gersh. Gersh does not name his suburb, but if it *is* Levittown, his impressions conflict with Wattel's findings.

[10] Samuel Lubell, *The Future of American Politics*, pp. 62-63.

character has been behind the apparent voting shift in suburbia. Whyte, for example, suggests that "A Democratic allegiance is part of an environment which the newcomers [to suburbia] wish to leave behind, and in attuning themselves to the values of the group they now wish to join, they soon find that 'acceptance,' to use a favorite word of suburbia, is more difficult if one persists in obdurately sticking to what others regard as a lower-class habit." [11]

Although it is certainly true that, generally speaking, the higher one's income level the greater the probability is that one will vote Republican, it seems rather to stretch a point to identify, or, more accurately, to say that others identify Democratic voting as a lower-class habit. Clearly, large numbers of people at the middle socioeconomic levels are liberal Democrats of the New Deal type, and by no stretch of the imagination could be called "lower class." Kornhauser *et al.* cite figures from the University of Michigan's national survey of the 1952 election which revealed that there was a larger percentage of Eisenhower votes among those earning less than $4,000 a year than among those earning between $4,000 and $5,000 a year.[12]

Indeed, a close look at the "anxiety to conform" thesis rapidly decreases whatever plausibility it might originally have had. For one thing, the new tract suburbs are *new*. Characteristically, they are rapidly occupied. If most of the new residents are former urban Democrats, then there would be no previously Republican ethos to which to conform. The attitudes that the new residents bring with them into the tract would presumably have at least as much effect upon their political behavior as the fact that the tract was constructed in a previously rural or "fringe" area predominantly Republican in character. Campbell *et al.* say that the great majority of "party attachments are lasting and unchanging. A large majority (of their national sample) deny ever having

[11] William H. Whyte, Jr., *op. cit.*, p. 332.
[12] See Arthur Kornhauser, *et al.*, *When Labor Votes*, p. 278, and Angus Campbell, *et al.*, *The Voter Decides*, pp. 70-73 for a demographic breakdown of the 1952 presidential vote. The majority of skilled and semiskilled workers who voted for Stevenson probably accounts for much of the increase in Stevenson votes in the $4,000 to $5,000 group over the less than $4,000 groups.

thought of themselves as belonging to the party other than the one of their current choice." [13] And even further, if suburbanites are as civically aware and active and organization-prone as many of the commentators on suburbia say they are, then there seems very little reason to suppose that suburbanites would be very vulnerable to the ministrations of the pre-tract Republican county organization. On the other hand, if the tract residents come from Republican backgrounds and continue to vote Republican after they become suburbanites, no one will be surprised. The point is that none of this seems to have anything to do with suburbia, as such.[14]

Perhaps the most elaborate explanation of the alleged suburban Republican trend is given by Louis Harris.[15] Harris's explanation, however elaborately stated, is essentially a simple one. Social mobility is the key; for Harris, like Whyte, suburbia is a melting pot in which the children and grandchildren of urban immigrants mix with older American stock, and emerge with white-collar aspirations. The common bond is a commitment to be modern, enlightened, moderate. A combination of political circumstances in 1952 —mainly the discrediting of the Democratic party by scandal and the dominance of the Republican party in suburbs: "Everyone knew that the town had an eight-to-one Republican registration. How was one to fight politically, except to join the modern, enlightened, and moderate wing of the Republican party?" (p. 122)— drove them to Eisenhower rather than to Stevenson. Harris analyzes the reasons that white-collar persons went Republican, and then concludes "a new balance of power had been born: the suburb" (p. 125). His analysis has to do with the social and economic position and aspirations of white-collar people; his conclusion has to do with suburbs. To what extent these two variables are coextensive is precisely the question that has been ignored.

---

[13] Angus Campbell, *et al., op. cit.*, p. 111.

[14] Indeed, the propensity to speak of a "suburban vote" may be a meaningless extension of the "place theory" implied in speaking of a "rural vote" or "urban vote." The political relevance of the two latter terms is not based simply on the fact that one group lives in the city whereas the other lives in the country; the rural-urban distinction is a social-economic-cultural distinction, and without any doubt, suburban tracts are typically urban culturally: their residents are not farmers, not isolated, not tradition oriented and so forth.

[15] See Louis Harris, *Is There a Republican Majority?*, pp. 118-139; for the quotations, see p. 122, 125.

Clearly, a test case of the effect of suburban residence on voting would be an examination of the political attitudes and behavior of previously urban Democrats who become suburbanites, *with other factors* held constant. Presumably it would not come as a great illumination to discover that a self-made, suddenly rich man would change his political loyalties in accord with radically altered interests, or even that a mobile organization-man, the son of an immigrant Democrat, would change his political loyalties in accord with his bright prospects. The key question is whether a modest improvement in one's standard of living as represented by a shift from old run-down urban neighborhoods to new suburbs by itself involves a political shift also. And, indeed, there is some evidence to suggest that these changes in political affiliation do not take place. The query of Lubell's respondent ("Why should I change?") reflects Campbell's finding, and is apparently echoed by the residents of Levittown, Pennsylvania. Indeed, one of the central questions posed by the Kornhauser study of the political behavior of auto workers was: "Can working people attain comfortable and respectable middle-class planes of living and yet persist in their loyalty to organized labor and labor's political aims?" [16] Although Kornhauser and his colleagues are cautious in answering this question, they are willing to commit themselves to the proposition that "Our study of auto workers contributes rather striking evidence that it is possible for wage earners to experience vast social and economic gains and yet remain steadfastly union oriented in their political views. This may well be the most significant of our findings." This conclusion applies not only to voting behavior in relation to income. Those auto workers who *lived* in higher income neighborhoods voted more strongly for Stevenson than those living in lower income neighborhoods. In addition, to the question of whether workers will take on middle-class social attitudes "as their status more closely approximates that of the white-collar classes, as they become homeowners, stockholders, suburbanites," the Kornhauser study gives a qualifiedly negative answer.[17]

In many respects, our findings tend to confirm those of Korn-

---

[16] Arthur Kornhauser, *et al.*, *op. cit.*, p. 274.
[17] *Ibid.*, pp. 278, 281, 283-284.

hauser, Sheppard, and Mayer. Of our sample, 81 per cent identified themselves as Democrats, 11 per cent as Republicans, and 6 per cent as independents; 2 per cent didn't know. The statistics on voting behavior are similarly unambiguous. Appendix table A.5 summarizes the total sample's voting record in the past three presidential elections. It is interesting to notice here that although Eisenhower did pick up a few votes among the non-Republicans in 1956, he picked up more in 1952—when these voters were members of the urban working class, and not suburbanites. In terms of *those who voted,* Eisenhower received 26 per cent of the vote in 1952; in 1956 he had not quite 18 per cent. On the basis of these figures alone, we could conclude that the Democratic vote has *increased* since the move to the suburbs.

The hypothesis that homeownership, by sensitizing the householder to taxes and by making him aware of his status as an owner of property, is in general a conservative influence leading him to become a Republican is not confirmed by our data. Appendix table A.6 shows that the percentage of those owning homes before the move who are Democrats is identical with the percentage of Democrats for the sample as a whole. Similarly, the suggestion that the political character of the area before occupancy of the new suburb will become the dominant political character of the new suburb is also not confirmed. San Jose and Santa Clara County in general are quite Republican in character. Santa Clara County gave 59.6 per cent of its vote to Eisenhower in 1952 and 58.9 per cent in 1956. Indeed, very little that is surprising emerges from cross tabulating political identification and voting with variables such as job, place of birth, religion, and so forth. It is true, for example, that a somewhat larger percentage of the foremen identified themselves as Republicans than the sample as a whole, but that was to be expected; a larger percentage of the "other Protestants" [18] identified themselves as Republicans than the Catholics, the Baptists, or those who identified themselves only as "Protestants." Similarly, a somewhat higher proportion of the rural born are Democrats than of the urban born, but this too is to be ex-

---

[18] The "other Protestants" include all those Protestants who identified themselves by denominations *other than* Baptist. The category excludes those who identified themselves simply as "Protestants"—not giving any denominational affiliation.

pected since most of these rural people are Southern rural. None of these minor variations, however, even came close to threatening the Democratic majority in any of the classifications.

One variable, however, that does seem clearly to affect political identity and behavior is age. Although the Democratic majorities are still not threatened, appendix table A.6 shows that the youngest and the oldest age groups are more heavily Republican than the age groups in between. This may be because most of both the youngest and the oldest group came to maturity in an era of Republican domination, whereas most of the two groups in between are children of the depression. The age group under 30 voted overwhelmingly for Eisenhower in 1952, but, inexplicably, voted just as overwhelmingly for Stevenson in 1956. There is no way in which we can account for this complete reversal except to refer to the well-documented instability of the ballots of young voters, and to the fact that in 1952 many of this group were probably in the midst of or fresh from military service and might have been attracted to Eisenhower because of this. In 1956, on the other hand, they were members of the U.A.W. These, however, are *ad hoc* hypotheses.

In all three elections for which data were collected, the proportion of the vote going to the Democratic candidate decreased as education increased; almost, but not quite as clearly, the Republican vote increased as education increased. Only among high school graduates, however, and only in the 1952 election, did the Republican presidential candidate receive more votes than the Democratic candidate. Of those with a high school education or more, 46 per cent are in the 20-29-year-old age group, but this fact does not raise any questions of spurious relationships between either of these two groups and voting. Clearly both age *and* education affect voting, but the small size of the sample prevented further statistical breakdowns to document to *what extent* this is true.

Appendix table A.7 shows clearly the increased strength of Stevenson in 1956, as compared with 1952—that is, after the move to the suburb. It is true that the group with an eighth grade education or less gave a very slightly smaller *proportion* of their vote to Stevenson in 1956 than they did in 1952, but on the whole I

think it can be safely said that, both in terms of political identifications and voting, this new tract suburb is a Democratic community, and that not only has the Republican vote not increased
among the workers since the move to the suburb, it has actually
decreased. And it has decreased in spite of the fact that the tract
is in a heavily Republican county.

There is, however, some evidence to suggest that homeownership contributes to an increased interest in politics—not to an
increased propensity toward *Republican* politics, but only toward
politics in general. Although interest in politics among the sample
as a whole is quite low (9 per cent very interested, 38 per cent
moderately interested, and 53 per cent hardly interested at all),
29 per cent reported that their interest in politics has increased
since the move to the suburb; 6 per cent reported that their interest in politics had decreased. I attribute this reported increase to
homeownership rather than to anything else because although
interest in politics was *highest* among those who owned homes
before the move to the suburbs (see appendix table A.8), the
percentage reporting an *increase* in interest in politics was *lowest*
in this group, as is indicated in appendix table A.9. Also consistent
with a general finding that it is the most depressed group (for
example, the former residents of the government housing) who
have been most clearly affected by the move to the suburb, is the
finding that it was the least educated (those with an eighth grade
education or less) who reported the largest percentage of increased interest in politics.[19]

Although our data clearly show that there has been some increased interest in politics, there is considerable doubt about the
actual extent to which this reported interest is manifested in political awareness and political activity. For one thing, only three
respondents reported having engaged in any party activity; one of
these was a foreman, a definite "city father" type who had run
(successfully) for election to the local school board; the other two

---

[19] Thirty-four per cent of the eighth graders reported increased interest in
politics. For the 9-11 grade group the figure is 25 per cent and for the high school
graduates the figure is 27 per cent. See chapter IV for analogous effects upon
religious interest.

were the president of the local union,[20] and a union representative
in the plant, both of whom can be said to have a kind of "professional" interest in politics. In addition, although the neighborhood
in which the interviewing was done is overwhelmingly Democratic,[21] only 50 per cent of the sample were able to identify the
community correctly as a primarily Democratic one. Although
only 4 per cent identified the community as primarily Republican,
15 per cent replied that it was about half Democratic and half
Republican, and 31 per cent were not willing to guess the dominant political character of the suburb. Further, to the question
inquiring as to the political affiliations of the two closest friends
of the respondents, 13 per cent did not know whether their two
closest friends were Republicans, Democrats, or independents,
and an additional 11 per cent were unable to identify the political
affiliation of *one* of their two closest friends.[22] And in explaining
their lack of knowledge of the political identities of their close
friends, some offered the opinion that politics, like religion, was
something that was better not discussed among friends.[23] In short,
the fact that there is little political activity, the fact that half of
the respondents did not know that the community was heavily
Democratic, and the fact that a substantial minority did not know
the politics of their close friends and felt that politics should not
be discussed among friends suggest that the evidence of increased
interest in politics may be only a subjective feeling which has not
yet been manifested. This lack of active interest in politics is further indicated by the fact that 80 per cent of the total sample
answered in the negative to the question of whether there were
any organizations whose political opinions they generally trusted.
On the other hand, the strong Democratic bias is indicated by the
fact that of the 20 who answered yes, 19 specified the union. The

---

[20] He said to me, "There's no advantage in trying to get ahead with Ford; I'm
a union man and have been a union supporter for fifteen years. Politics have
always been a part of my life."

[21] The district registrar of voters (a Ford engineer), who turned up in the pre-
test sample, informed me that the tract was about 80 per cent Democratic.

[22] Out of 200 friends, 125 were identified as Democrats, 34 as Republicans, 4 as
independents; 37 could not be politically identified.

[23] One respondent spoke for more than merely himself when he commented
darkly, "We don't talk politics around here."

other one mentioned an ethnic organization in which he is active.

The Democratic bias of this group of suburbanites runs through their entire families. The wives of the respondents are only slightly less overwhelmingly Democratic than their husbands, and the vote of the wives for Eisenhower in 1956 was only 2 per cent higher than the vote of their husbands. The percentage of non-voters among the wives is much higher than among the husbands. Further, they come from Democratic families; out of 200 parents, 133 were counted as Democrats, 30 as Republicans, and 19 as independents; the politics of 8 parents was unknown, and the rest never lived in the United States.

In conclusion, then, we can say that this particular move to suburbia has not produced a Republican tendency in previously Democratic voters. What increased interest in politics was reported seems to be a function of homeownership, although there is some doubt about the actual extent of *active* interest in politics. In addition, not only has a tendency to Republicanism not been evident, but the increased interest in politics has taken place *only* among the Democrats and the independents. Appendix table A.9 shows clearly not only that the Republicans have not reported any increased interest in politics, but that they were the only group with considerably less interest than they had earlier. The small number of Republicans in the sample prevents us from saying anything really conclusive about them, but apparently the over-whelmingly Democratic composition of their neighborhood seems to have dampened to some extent their interest in politics. An analogous phenomenon is that the Republicans show considerably less interest than the Democrats in union affairs. None of the Republicans goes to union meetings even "occasionally." More than half of them say they "never" go. Of the Democrats, on the other hand, 17 per cent say they go "occasionally" and 9 per cent "often." Of course, it is not possible to say whether this implies that Democrats in Republican suburbs will have their interest in politics dampened, but there does seem to be considerable doubt that simply moving into a suburban tract can by itself change habits which, like voting, go emotionally deep.

Still, it would be misleading simply to end this chapter on a negative note. More important than the negative fact that these suburbanites have not gone Republican are the positive facts that their suburban experience has apparently both increased their Democratic preference and contributed to their increasing subjective interest in politics. These facts confirm Kornhauser's assertion that auto workers can experience vast social and economic gains and yet still remain working class in their outlook and their political loyalties. It seems to me that this is possible because these "gains" are *collective* gains; they were not achieved in the classic American manner, by capitalizing on the tradition of *individual* opportunity. Consequently, it would be misleading to conceive of the phenomenon in the traditional terms of social mobility; and without this, of course, we have no reason to expect them to act like "suburbanites." But to say this is only to reveal the inadequacy of the current image of the suburbanite, because our respondents *are* suburbanites in the only realistic sense in which the term can be used. It is the fact that they are wage workers which makes the situation interesting. The behavior that Whyte reports in Park Forest and other suburbs like it is, after all, only a large scale version of the behavior of socially mobile, middle-class families, which has been familiar to sociologists for many years. The vast increases in the proportion of the labor force in white-collar occupations (proportions which are increasingly suburban in residence) certainly justify the great amounts of interest shown by sociologists and other students of cultural trends in the development of the "suburban way of life." But the movement of the urban middle class to suburbia seems, from the many reports on life in such suburbs, to be an extension of urban middle-class culture to a suburban context, and not really a "new" way of life. The *new* phenomenon is not middle-class suburbia, but rather the achievement by large numbers of *wage workers* of incomes permitting them to buy new houses in the suburbs. The question at hand is whether or not they will take on the style of the suburban middle class or *extend* their own style to the suburbs—as the middle class has done. Our data indicate that the latter is closer to the truth of what is happening.

Chapter IV

Has There Been a Return to Religion in Suburbia?

One of the most remarkable developments in the postwar period of prosperity in the United States has been the apparent upsurge in religion. Statistics on virtually every index by which the status of religion is measured, have been cited to demonstrate that Americans are becoming more and more religious. Figures on belief in God, denominational identification, church attendance, church construction, and the status of clergymen have all been used to argue that a "return to religion" has occurred on a mass basis. Will Herberg, the prominent Jewish theologian, concludes: "That there has in recent years been an upswing of religion can hardly be doubted; the evidence is diverse, converging, and unequivocal beyond all possibilities of error." [1] Almost equally unambiguous is the belief that suburbia is the primary locus of the contemporary return to religion; that is to say, it is in the new tract suburbs that we can see most clearly manifested the increasing importance of religion in American life. At the very least, the new suburbs are communities "in which the churches are more important institutions than anyone who was

---

[1] Will Herberg, *Protestant, Catholic, Jew*, p. 69. See chapter iv of this book, "The Contemporary Upswing in Religion," pp. 59-84, and particularly pp. 62-63 for citations of much of the statistical evidence of the upswing. See also Leo Rosten (ed.), *A Guide to the Religions of America*, pp. 236-248.

brought up in the twenties or thirties would have imagined they would be." [2] Apparently, the increased importance of the church in suburbia is related to the manifold functions it performs there. In his interview survey of suburbia, Harry Henderson noted that

Churches were the first major organizations to be set up in most [suburban] communities. . . . Nearly every family interviewed reported that they felt the need for churches immediately and deeply in these communities. . . . Churches in these communities provide for many needs: social activity, group identification, family counseling, and spiritual security. . . . Many people reported their own religious feelings have deepened "because living here you realize the importance and truth of the church's teaching." [3]

Indeed, it is precisely the feeling that the suburban church fulfills so many needs that has made a number of students of suburbia, including churchmen, doubt the genuineness of the "return to religion." "One comes early to get a seat in suburban churches; they overflow and new ones are being built every day. One would think this would make clergymen crow with delight. Some do, but many are shaking their heads gloomily." [4] The gloom comes from an apprehension that the evidence of the religious upswing has more social and cultural than spiritual significance; that it is not religion but religiosity that is on the increase; that the values behind the alleged "upswing" are eminently secular, not sacred. David Riesman suggests that although the increasing church attendance in the new suburbs comes "occasionally out of a genuine religious call" it is more likely to be due to an urge "to be respectable or to climb socially" and "even more typically because the church, like the high school and the country club, has become a center for the family as a social and civic unit." [5] Riesman's statement is characteristically mild; characteristically extreme but saying essentially the same thing is the statement in *The Nation:*

The main mood of many a suburban church on Sundays is that of a fashionable shopping center. . . . On weekdays one shops for food, on Saturdays one shops for recreation and on Sundays one shops for

---

[2] Frederick Lewis Allen, "The Big Change in Suburbia," p. 26.

[3] Harry Henderson, "Rugged American Collectivism, The Mass-Produced Suburbs, Part II," p. 82.

[4] Stanley Rowland, Jr., "Suburbia Buys Religion," p. 78.

[5] David Riesman, "The Suburban Dislocation," p. 132.

the Holy Ghost. . . . The suburban church . . . is accepted by the mass as no more than a pleasing and fashionable facet of culture. . . . The House of the Lord is being reduced to a comfort station.[6]

Lest we think that these are the prejudiced perceptions of secularists, we have the testimony of Herberg himself that

> . . . it is not difficult to see the current turn to religion and the church as . . . a reflection of the growing other-directedness of our middle class culture. The people in the suburbs want to feel psychologically secure. . . . Being religious and joining a church is, under contemporary American conditions, a fundamental way of "adjusting" and "belonging." . . . The vogue of van Gogh and Renoir reproductions in the suburban home and the rising church affiliation of the suburban community may not be totally unconnected. . . . The trend toward religious identification and church affiliation may thus to an extent be a reflection of the growing need for conformity and sociability. . . .[7]

That this is as true for Jews as for Christians is indicated by testimony of a rabbi from a New York suburb: "Most of my new congregation are new to synagogue experience. . . . In the city it takes an effort to become a member. . . . But out here it's the path of least resistance." [8]

In addition to "worrying about keeping his church big enough for his flock," the suburban clergyman apparently has considerably more than a full-time job on his hands in ministering to the personal problems of his parishioners.

> So many Lakewooders are young couples lately liberated from the proximity of their families, that the Rev. Harold S. Carlson, 34, pastor of the First Baptist Church, used to spend two-thirds of his time on marriage counseling. He now has an assistant pastor who does nothing else.[9]

The frequency with which remarks like this appear in the literature almost makes one apprehensive that the divorce rate is about to spurt upward again. William Whyte quotes one of his clergy-

---

[6] Rowland, *op. cit.*, pp. 79-80.
[7] Herberg, *op. cit.*, pp. 72-73.
[8] Quoted by Harry Gersh, "The New Suburbanites of the 50's," p. 219. Apparently, from Gersh's analysis, suburban Jews, no longer in a ghetto, seek the synagogue as a way of finding a Jewish community in the suburb where they are no longer a majority, as they were, say, in the Bronx.
[9] "The New America: Living Atop a Civic Mushroom," *Newsweek* (April 1, 1957), p. 37.

man-respondents as saying, "So many young people around here makes counseling my main worry. . . . I simply haven't time for any more, and I am getting an assistant to help me out." [10] And Henderson quotes still another clergyman as saying, "I would say that we ministers here [in the suburbs] give three, perhaps four times as much time to marital problems as ministers do elsewhere." [11]

If Whyte and others are right when they say that what suburbanites want most of all out of their religion is a sense of community, then it is not surprising that they seem to be caring less and less about matters of doctrine that might impede its achievement. "Acclimation to suburbia," says Whyte, "stimulates switches in religious affiliation, and the couple from, say, a small Ozark town is likely to discard their former fundamentalist allegiance to become Methodists or Presbyterians." [12] Echoing Whyte is the statement by Seeley and his colleagues that Crestwood Heights families may shed their religious beliefs when they are experienced as cumbersome or obsolete. They "cannot afford to be held back by old fashioned beliefs any more than . . . to be tied to old fashioned people. . . . Like a new and finer house, a new and advanced religion can be a powerful source of reassurance to the Crestwooder that he has escaped his hampering past and can now grasp at a more alluring and dazzling future." [13]

In summary, three distinct but related questions have been raised: has there been a widespread return to religion in the United States in recent years? is this return most evident in the new suburbs? and third, does the return to religion really signify a spiritual reawakening or only a heightened awareness by suburbanites of the role of religion in creating "the new roots," that is, a stable, ordered life in the prosperous United States? These questions show every promise of developing into something approaching the intensity (and the ambiguity) of the question of whether or not the stratification system of the United States is becoming more rigid. In any case, some have doubted what Herberg says "can hardly be doubted," namely, that there *has* been a

---

[10] William H. Whyte, Jr., *The Organization Man*, p. 420.
[11] Harry Henderson, *op. cit.*, p. 82.
[12] Whyte, *op. cit.*, p. 333.
[13] John Seeley *et al.*, *Crestwood Heights*, pp. 215-216.

massive return to religion. A recent article by S. M. Lipset, for example, examines comparative data on church affiliation, church attendance, the ratio of clergy to population, the ratio of available church seats to population, and the religious beliefs of college students, and concludes that "Such statistical data as we have examined . . . all argue against the thesis that religious practice in America in the mid-twentieth century is at its high point," that, indeed, during the past hundred years "there has been little change in the strength of institutionalized religion." [14] Yet in spite of Lipset's work, the evidence is still ambiguous. Lipset, for example, cites the reports of mid-nineteenth-century European travelers in the United States to the effect that America was then and still is the most religious country in the West. But since the alleged turn *away* from religion did not initially occur until around the turn of the century (presumably as a function of urbanization and industrialization), the comparison is not as revealing as it might be. Similarly, Lipset's citation of the increasing number of college students who do not believe in God is countered by the Gallup reports that college-educated people go to church more often than those with less education.[15] The whole issue, of course, is complicated by the unreliability of many of the statistics on church affiliation and church attendance, but it does seem premature to dismiss the testimony of so many observers regarding the return to religion, particularly in suburbia. The question is still an open one, and what is needed is more detailed research on the relation between certain demographic variables and the propensity toward religious activity. One familiar hypothesis, for example, is that social mobility, by uprooting people from their traditional ways of life, has the initial effect of weakening traditional religious ties and observations. I do not say that this is so (although there is some evidence to support it), but only that it is premature to dismiss the hypothesis as facile, since it may help to explain the virtual unanimity with which students of new white-collar suburbs report the return to religion there. There may be a point beyond which the psychological strains of social mobility dictate a search for the security which a return to the church may provide. Surely,

[14] Seymour Martin Lipset, "Trends in American Society"; see also his "What Religious Revival?" *Columbia University Forum,* Winter, 1959, p. 20.
[15] See Rosten, *op. cit.,* p. 241.

this is the appeal which the evangelist Billy Graham has used with such extraordinary success, and with which countless popular religious books have achieved the status of best seller.[16]

Nevertheless, the new suburb under analysis here is not a white-collar suburb, and our data indicate that there has been no marked increase in religious participation for the sample considered as a whole. Appendix table A.10, for example, shows that 56 per cent of the sample attend church never or rarely, and the figures as a whole suggest that these suburbanites attend church *less* often than the national average as reported in the Gallup poll of March 26, 1954.[17] The fact that 28 per cent of the wives go to church more often than their husbands is entirely consistent with the fact that women generally go to church more often than men. Living in the new tract suburb has apparently had little clear effect upon the frequency of church attendance of our sample. Almost as many go to church less often in this suburb as go more often, but the largest percentage (49) have not had their church attendance affected in any marked way. It is true, of course, that 51 per cent *have* had the frequency of their church attendance affected, but the fact that 27 per cent have been affected one way whereas 24 per cent have been affected another way indicates that the influence of suburban residence on church attendance is not a uniform one.

Low percentages turn up not only for the question of church attendance but for other indices of religious participation as well. Participation in church activities other than attendance at Sunday services is practically nil; 81 per cent of the sample said they "never" participated. And in spite of the plaints of the ministers quoted by Whyte, Henderson, and *Newsweek* about the amount

---

[16] At the other extreme, and with a much more sophisticated formulation but dealing with a similar problem is the complex phenomenon of the return of many intellectuals (mobile men *par excellence*) to the church, a favorite topic of discussion among intellectuals. In 1949, *Partisan Review* thought the problem real enough to run a symposium lasting through many issues on "Religion and the Intellectuals."

[17] Gallup asked a national sample whether they had been to church within the last seven days. Fifty-three per cent reported they had; 47 per cent reported they had not. See Rosten, *op. cit.*, p. 239. The disparity is hardly surprising in light of the facts that white-collar persons go to church more often than blue-collar persons and people in the far west go to church less often than people in any other section of the country. *Ibid.*, pp. 239-241.

of time they have to devote to family and marital problems, 93 per cent of our sample reported that they had never spoken to their clergyman about any of their family problems, and this percentage was no larger or smaller in the suburb than before the move. Indeed, the 93 per cent might have been higher, because three of the seven who did report having sought their clergymen for counsel did so only because they were planning to marry a woman of a different faith. In short, there was no marked tendency by these suburbanites to become involved in church activity.

When religious participation was considered in subgroups of our sample, relatively few clear trends were apparent. For example, appendix table A.10 shows that the percentage of those who never go to church increased with increased education.[18] But whereas there is a 15 per cent spread between the least educated and the most educated in the "never" category, this drops to a 4 per cent spread when the "never" and "rarely" categories are combined.[19] Similarly ambiguous results emerge when church attendance is cross tabulated by type of former residence. Again, there is a 15 per cent spread between those who lived in the government housing projects in Richmond and those who rented private apartments—both in the "never" category and in the "every Sunday" category. The church attendance of the former homeowners is not remarkably high, and, oddly enough, the most frequent church attendance is manifested by the former residents of the government housing in Richmond. This is contrary to all expectations because the former residents of the government housing constitute, as a group, perhaps the most depressed and disorganized of the subgroups with which we are dealing, and church attendance is supposed to drop the further down the class hierarchy one goes. Perhaps it is precisely because the *contrast* between their former living conditions and their present ones is

---

[18] This finding is contrary to national samples, which show that the higher one's education the more likely one is to attend church frequently. But our finding may be spurious because almost half of those with a high school education or more are less than 30 years old, and religious participation is known to rise markedly after age 30.

[19] In this and other cross tabulations of church attendance, there is a marked tendency for the figures to bunch at the extremes. Apparently, people go to church hardly ever or else very often, with relatively few in between. This is contrary to what we would normally expect.

most marked among this group that not only do they attend church most frequently but it is also they who constitute the heaviest proportion of those who reported that they go to church more often in the suburb than they did in Richmond. Appendix table A.12 shows that it is *only* this group which, as a whole, reported a net increase in its church attendance since the move to the suburbs. The new impact of religion on this group is further emphasized when we remember that although 27 per cent of the total sample reported that they go to church more often, and 24 per cent reported that they go less often, 42 per cent of the total sample reported that the *community as a whole* goes to church more frequently than their former communities, whereas only 22 per cent reported that the suburban community as a whole goes less often. But the breakdown of these data in appendix table A.12 shows that the former residents of the government housing projects are the *only* ones who characterized the suburb in any striking way as a more churchgoing community than their former communities, and the magnitude of the figure is extreme. We should add, however, that selective factors in perception are clearly at work in judging the amount of churchgoing that characterizes the suburb. Appendix table A.12, for example, also strikingly documents the fact that those who themselves go to church more often in the suburb perceive the suburb as a more churchgoing community, and vice versa.

Also revealing are the breakdowns on church participation by denominational identification. The only religious group which showed a marked propensity toward churchgoing were the Baptists. In the part of appendix table A.10 which represents church attendance by denomination, we see that only 32 per cent of the Baptists never or rarely go to church, whereas the figure is 56 per cent for the sample as a whole. Also, 59 per cent of the Baptists go to church often or every Sunday whereas the figure for the sample as a whole is only 30 per cent. Notice that the "Protestants," that is, those who would not specify any denomination, constitute almost one-quarter of the total sample, and are virtually nonchurchgoers. Very few of the Catholics, on the other hand, said they never went to church, but more than 40 per cent of them go to church rarely, so that if the two categories are combined, they closely approach the figures for the sample as a whole. The "other Protestants," that is, those who identified themselves by denominations other than Baptist, conform most closely to the figures for the total sample.

The Baptists are the only group which go to church more often in the suburb than they did in their former neighborhoods. Appendix table A.11 shows not only this, but also the remarkable balance of the other groups, with exception of the Catholics, who go to church somewhat less often in the suburb than in their former neighborhoods. The fact that the Baptists and the former residents of the government housing are the only groups who go to church relatively often and who go to church *more* often in the suburb than before, suggests some relation between being a Baptist and having lived in the government housing projects. And that is precisely what we find: 59 per cent of the Baptists lived in the government projects immediately before the move (the figure for the sample as a whole is 38 per cent), and the Baptists constituted 33 per cent of our sample of the former residents of the government housing—the largest denomination represented. As a matter of fact, the consistency with which the Baptists account for most of the church activity of our sample is rather startling. Thus, whereas only 7 per cent of the total sample have discussed their family problems with suburban clergymen, 14 per cent of the Baptists have. Whereas only 7 per cent of the total sample engaged in church activities often (other than attendance at Sunday services), 23 per cent of the Baptists did. Sixteen per cent of the total sample felt that the church had become more important to them since the move to the suburbs, but 41 per cent of the Baptists felt this way. I say that all this is rather startling because the pattern of church activity that emerges from the data suggests that it is the *least* advantaged groups which manifest most religious interest and activity. As we saw, almost 60 per cent of the Baptists were former residents of the government housing projects —formerly the most poorly housed of our respondents. In addition, it was the most poorly educated who attended church most frequently; it is this least educated group also who participate most often in other church activities: 24 per cent of those with an eighth grade education or less participated "sometimes" or "often" in "other church activities," compared to 8 per cent of those with more than an eighth grade education. Similarly, 21 per cent of the least educated group felt that the church had become more important to them since the move to the suburbs; only 12 per cent of those with more than an eighth grade education felt this way. Again, it is the semiskilled production line workers who show a greater propensity toward church activity than the skilled workers, the foremen, and the non-line workers.[20]

Although there has been no marked over-all "return to religion" in the suburb under discussion, I fully expected (in line with the reports on white-collar suburbs) that what evidence there *was* of a religious upswing would be most apparent in those groups which most closely approximate white-collar status, that is, the well educated, the higher status workers, the former homeowners, and, of course, the group less than 30 years old (because this group is both relatively well educated and relatively mobile in its expectations). But none of this is true. Appendix table A.10 shows not only that the 20- to 29-year old group does not go to church any more often than the other groups; 45 per cent of them do not go at all. What is true is that the most obvious pattern is for the lowest status groups to manifest most religious interest and activity. Now this may be owing in part to the overrepresentation in the sample of former "Bible-belt Baptists" who, presumably, have carried their strong religious tradition with them. But also relevant, I think, is the fact that the *contrast* between their former living conditions and their present ones is most marked in this group; in Richmond, whether as government housing residents or not, the "Okies" and the "Arkies" were never welcomed by the old residents, and if they were government housing residents, they lived in a virtual slum and under perpetual threat of eviction, since tearing down the housing projects to free the land on which they stood for industrial use was a primary aim of the Richmond redevelopment plan. In the suburb, on the other hand, everyone is a newcomer, no one lives in a slum, no one is under threat of

---

[20] The only deviation from this pattern of relationship between socioeconomic disadvantage and high religious interest and activity is the fact that those who were homeowners before the move participate somewhat more frequently in "other church activities" than do the former government renters.

eviction, and everyone's standard of living is approximately at the same comfortable level. It is not at all unlikely, therefore, that those for whom the move to the suburbs represents the greatest *difference* vis-à-vis their former material level of existence should be most affected on the cultural level. But I wish to emphasize both that the cultural effect does not necessarily mean that they are becoming "middle class," and *especially* that the cultural consequences of the move *are not evenly distributed throughout the different dimensions of cultural behavior.* For example, although their political and religious interest does seem to have increased somewhat, there is no evidence to suggest that the increase is dominated by status considerations. And at the same time (as we shall see) the increase in political and religious interest is not matched by increases in formal or informal social participation nor in "improved" tastes.

In any case, our primary intent here is not to account statistically for the variations in religious activity in the subgroups of the sample, but rather to suggest that there is little in our overall findings to support either the notion that suburbs as such are the locus of a massive return to religion,[21] or that whatever religious "return" there has been is essentially a secular phenomenon.

Nevertheless, fears that religious observance in the new suburbs is only an aspect of conformity, a kind of shopping for roots or a search for sociability, continue to grow among churchmen and laymen alike. A Roman Catholic priest, for example, can write: "It may be possible to sit in an air-conditioned ranch house and watch a color television set and still not be attached to the things of this world. It may, in short, be possible to harmonize the world of the gadget and the world of the spirit. All these things are possible, but they are not easy."[22] And a Protestant, fearing the

---

[21] Excluding the foremen, who are not members of the union, almost one-quarter of the sample said that the union was more important to the welfare of their families than the church. This seems to be an extraordinary admission. An additional 12 per cent found the question too difficult to answer.

[22] Andrew Greeley, "The Catholic Suburbanite," p. 31. Father Greeley, in explaining his fears for the future of Catholicism in the suburbs, cites the melting pot thesis and makes the interesting observation that, with the spread of education and the general raising of the level of culture, the parish priest is no longer necessarily either the best educated or the wisest member of the Catholic community—which, of course, reflects upon his status.

"capture" of the church by "suburban values," writes: " . . . suburbia expresses most fully the secularization of life which has accompanied industrialization. It represents the final step in the secularization of the church and in the isolation of Christianity from man's struggle for bread." [23] Surely, there is something curiously old-fashioned or nostalgic about comments like these. Father Greeley apparently believes that a high standard of living makes it difficult for one to be truly religious, and Winter's remark suggests that the disappearance of the need to "struggle" for one's bread may be dealing Christianity a mortal blow. If Christianity is the religion of the poor, there may be some ground to these fears.[24] But with the development of what John Galbraith has recently called "the affluent society," religious ministering to the poor may just become an obsolete function. By itself, however, this would hardly seem to constitute any threat to religion; it is highly doubtful that, if pressed, either Greeley or Winter, despite their fears, would assert that the comfortable are not as good Christians as the wretched. In spite of Christ's remark about the camel and the eye of the needle, the rejection of opulence has been the exception in Christian practice, not the rule. On the other hand, there is every reason to expect a change in the *quality* of religious observance as standards of living rise on a mass scale; the churches of the wealthy have never been noted for the *fervor* of their communicants, and as ever larger numbers of people are raised out of economic misery we should not be surprised if their religious practice becomes milder or more "polite." But there is no reason to interpret a mild and polite approach to religion as fraudulent unless "genuine" religion is identified with Franciscan burlap and rope or the evangelist's fire and brimstone. As Durkheim noted over and over again, the power of religion is not due to the special nature of its religious conceptions, but rather to the fact

---

[23] Gibson Winter, "The Church in Suburban Captivity," p. 1113.

[24] The irony latent in the remarks of these churchmen is the apparent incipience of the view of religion as an opiate to deaden economic misery. Ironies like this are not limited to churchmen or even to the question of religion. Doctrinal movements whose appeal in large part is directed at a substantial *underprivileged* stratum seem nonplused at the gradual disappearance of such a stratum. Socialists, for example, seem to fear that high standards of living for workers will paralyze the working-class movement. See the discussion of this point in the concluding chapter of this study.

that it *is* a society. "What constitutes this society is the existence of a certain number of beliefs and practices common to all the faithful, traditional and thus obligatory. . . . The details of dogmas and rites are secondary. The essential thing is that they be capable of supporting a sufficiently intense collective life." [25] The functions of solidarity and security are thus properly inherent in religion. If this is true, then the moral basis of the apprehension of churchmen and laymen alike over the "genuineness" of the return to religion in suburbia is not at all clear. A respondent who said "The church helps you forget your troubles" and another respondent who said "Going to church makes you feel part of everything" seem to be experiencing two of the proper and universal functions of the religious life. On the other hand, many of today's commentators on suburbia are apt to interpret statements like these as variations on the dour theme of "conformity," wrinkle their brows, and fear for the future of religion in America.

With this analysis, I do not mean to suggest that religion may not be used cynically—as an avenue of social mobility or as a means toward respectability. I mean only to suggest that the secular *functions* of religion—perhaps particularly evident in white-collar suburbs—are not convincing evidence of the cynicism. Thus whatever logic there is to the fears of Protestant, Catholic, and Jewish leaders for the future of their churches in suburbia rests not in some obscure power that suburban residence has over the souls of men, but rather to the very plain and familiar power that the ideology of success has over the souls of Americans, and which only *sometimes* is legitimately symbolized by the image of suburbia. It is much safer to attack suburbia and worry fashionably about its dark influences than to attack the forces of which it is, after all, only a rather inaccurate symbol. [26] But in the largely homogeneous, working-class suburb which we have studied here, the pressures of mobility are largely absent; social

[25] Emile Durkheim, *Suicide*, p. 170. See also The Elementary Forms of the Religious Life, book iii, chapter vi, "Conclusion." It should be noted also that regardless of social background, the desire to participate in organized church activity seems to vary widely among individuals—even individuals of the same family.

[26] Wattel has remarked that ". . . much of the negative criticism aimed at suburbia should have been directed instead at our national culture." Harold L. Wattel, "Levittown: A Suburban Community," p. 287.

and civic activity is not very evident, and churchgoing does not, in general, provide oportunity for social climbing. What it apparently does provide, at least to the Baptists, is the partial recapture of the solidarity of their rural past; but it is a new kind of solidarity, rooted not in rural poverty but in suburban domestic comfort. Whether or not the new religious observance is *merely* a function of domestic comfort, bereft of a genuine reverence, it is, of course, not possible to say. But what Harry Gersh has said about the "return to religion" among suburban Jews seems generally applicable. "In all the above there is little mention of those who come to the synagogue because this is the place where Torah lives. But they are the minority in Suburbia, as they are everywhere." [27]

---

[27] Harry Gersh, *op. cit.*, p. 221.

Chapter V

Workers at Leisure:
Formal and Informal Participation

In spite of the accumulating evidence which suggests that "suburbia" is not a homogeneous phenomenon—neither the brave new
world incarnate conjured up by real estate men nor the intellectual's foam rubber trap apparently ready to snap shut—it is nevertheless widely believed that "There is a remarkable similarity in
attitudes toward politics, education, economics, sex, religion from
suburb to suburb. Almost a new way of life is in the making in
these comunities, and it is not a synthetic way of life 'sold' by mass
producers of suburbs." [1] Whyte is cautious enough to qualify by
saying "almost" a new way of life, but others are not so cautious.
Sylvia Fava has said, "There are no grounds for doubting that
suburbanism is a 'way of life' as well as an ecological phenomenon." [2] Father Greeley subtitles his essay on suburbia "A New
Way of Life," and Nathan Whetten has suggested that it is not
at all unlikely that "the really typical American of the future
will be found living in suburbia rather than in Main Street, Plain-
ville, or Middletown." [3]

At the heart of this new or almost new way of life seems to be

[1] William H. Whyte, Jr., "The Transients," p. 118.
[2] Sylvia Fava, "Suburbanism as a Way of Life," p. 37.
[3] Nathan Whetten, "Suburbanization as a Field for Sociological Research,"
p. 321.

the intimate communality of it. Whyte quotes his respondents as saying that life in the Park Forest suburb is like an army camp, or better yet, a fraternity house. No sooner does he enter the suburb than the new resident is suddenly "plunged into a hotbed of Participation. . . . Every minute from 7 A.M. to 10 P.M. some organization is meeting somewhere. . . . They [the suburbanites] hate it and they love it. Sometimes it seems that they are drawn to participation just for participation's sake." [4] That Whyte's observation is not a solitary one is evidenced by the comments of many others regarding the vitality of the organizational life in suburbia. "Nearly everyone belongs to organizations and, generally speaking, tries to be involved. . . . In addition to such service organizations as Lions and Kiwanis, there are clubs for every occupation and hobby. . . . The one organization to which everybody belongs is the Parent-Teachers association; its meetings are jammed and often loud with queries and arguments." [5] Henderson's observations are almost duplicated by Frederick Lewis Allen, who sees the new suburbs as "very gregarious communities, in which people wander in and out of one another's houses without invitation, and organize themselves into everything from car pools to PTA's and hobby clubs of numerous sorts." [6] Indeed, the frequency with which many of these writers echo each other is striking; where Henderson says they come and go without invitation, Whyte echoes "there isn't much privacy . . . in Park Forest . . . people don't bother to knock and they come and go furiously." [7]

All this furious coming and going apparently has some civic basis. One suburbanite, writing about his experience in suburbia, suggests that the "civic organization" is the source of the organized ties that people have to their neighbors. "The civic organiza-

[4] William H. Whyte, Jr., *The Organization Man*, pp. 317-318. "Abnormal? Or the portent of a new normality? The values of Park Forest, one gets the feeling, are harbingers of the way it's going to be." *Ibid.*, p. 311.
[5] Harry Henderson, "Rugged American Collectivism: The Mass Produced Suburbs, Part II," p. 81. "You will find lawyers arguing with lawyers, salesmen selling salesmen, photographers making prints, women sewing together; others are acting, making ceramics, building models of all sorts, singing, painting, even writing and reading aloud short stories—all as group activity. Nobody is expected to be an expert and everything is done with great enthusiasm." *Loc. cit.*
[6] Frederick Lewis Allen, "The Big Change in Suburbia, Part I," p. 26.
[7] Whyte, *op. cit.*, p. 389.

tion keeps an eye on tax rates, traffic on residential streets, and
exceptions to the zoning code. So we joined the civic organization.
The first time we sat with our next door neighbor. The next time
we sat with that couple who supported our stand on school taxes.
At the PTA we picked up a few more kindred souls. . . ." [8] But
this busy social life seems to have more than a civic or rational
basis; it has an ideological one too, and what Whyte calls the
"social ethic" is manifested, it seems, in the guilt people feel if
they do *not* participate in group activity in the new suburbs.
"Privacy has become clandestine. Not in solitary and selfish con-
templation but in doing things with other people does one fulfill
oneself. Nor is it a matter of overriding importance just what one
does with other people; even watching television together . . .
helps make one more of a real person." [9] Whyte, of course, is only
satirizing the semieducated vocabulary of his suburbanites by
his usage of "real person," for their explanations of their hyperactive, sociable behavior are shot through with phrases like "socio-
cultural groups" and the argot of the "life-adjustment" school of
thought (which has recently become a *bête noir* of the Luce
Magazines). Henderson cites one of his respondents as saying
that "the activity gives them 'self-expression' or 'new friends with
common interests' or 'an emotional outlet'; otherwise I'd take it
out on the kids." [10] At the same time, others are apparently having
second thoughts about the way in which neighborly love envelops
one in the suburbs. Whyte reports that one of the Park Forest
residents told him: "At the beginning we were maybe too neighborly—your friends knew more about your private life than you
did yourself! It's not quite that active now. But it's still real
friendy—even our dogs and cats are friendly with one another.
The street behind us is nowhere near as friendly. They knock on
doors over there." [11] In light of all this, David Riesman is being
eminently judicious when, comparing the evidence of hierarchical
status exclusion in places like Middletown, Yankee City, or Elmtown with the evidence of hierarchy in the new suburbs, he con-

---

[8] Harry Gersh, "The New Suburbanites of the 50's," p. 219.
[9] Whyte, *op. cit.*, p. 390.
[10] Henderson, *op. cit.*, p. 81.
[11] Whyte, *op. cit.*, p. 368.

cludes that "the new suburbanite appears to suffer less from exclusion than from a surfeit of inclusions." [12]
We have here, then, a series of testimonials that both formal and informal participation in the new suburbs is frequent enough and striking enough to constitute a definitive characteristic of the "suburban way of life." It is true, of course, that since Tocqueville, Americans have always been characterized as a nation of "joiners." The suburban evidence, however, seems to go beyond this stereotype; summarizing many of the recent studies, Max Lerner concludes that "recent experience shows that when people move from the . . . city to the . . . suburb, their participation in club and associational life increases deeply." [13] In addition to participation in organizations which, to one extent or another, are "formal," the evidence of high incidence of "informal" neighboring in the new suburbs is overwhelming. Lest one think that this evidence comes solely from impressions, Sylvia Fava has gone on record as saying that her research in Levittown, New York, supports the observation that the "suburban way of life" includes a "high degree of neighboring and other informal primary-type group contacts." [14] Walter Martin also gives apparent assent to Whyte's descriptions of lively mutual visiting or "neighboring" in suburbia.[15] Partygoing seems to be an important part of informal social relationships in the new suburbs, and worth mentioning separately. Although Newsweek does not cite its authorities, it has reported that "scientific observers have pegged Suburbia as an area of relatively high liquor consumption fostered by a multitude of neighborhood parties and other rites of sociability that sometimes border on the frantic." [16] One of Newsweek's authorities

---

[12] David Riesman, "The Suburban Dislocation," p. 124. Riesman grants that this is an impression based only upon a few cases. He suggests that studies of suburbs of smaller cities are sorely needed, since these impressions have been garnered from suburbs of our largest cities only.

[13] Max Lerner, America as a Civilization, p. 637.

[14] Sylvia Fava, op. cit., p. 37.

[15] "The lack of common interests and other differences which so frequently limit interaction between urban neighbors is thus likely to be missing in the suburbs. The 'neighboring' activities, 'kaffeeklatsches,' and almost frantic 'socializing' of the residents of the newer suburban areas have been graphically described." Walter T. Martin, "The Structuring of Social Relationships Engendered by Suburban Residence," p. 452.

[16] "The New Suburbia: Living Atop a Civic Mushroom," Newsweek (April 1, 1957), p. 37.

may be Mowrer of Northwestern (whom they cite in another context) or it may be Whyte, who, in one of his early articles, noted that "civic activity . . . is a fraction of the energy expended in group activities. . . . Social life throbs with bridge and canasta, bring-your-own-bottle parties, and teas; and when spring brings everyone outdoors, the tempo of activity becomes practically nonstop. 'Any excuse for a party' one resident says, happily." [17] Whyte apparently was not exaggerating, because a *Saturday Evening Post* writer, who took the trouble to check, reported that Park Forest families "give all sorts of parties. The list includes a Valentine costume party, surprise baby showers, PTA bunco party, progressive dinner party, picnics, Christmas-gift-exchange party, New Year's Eve party, bridge club, fish-house-punch party, breakfast after a dance, eggnog party before a Poinsettia ball, and a come-as-you-are birthday party." [18]

Now it is hardly news to sociologists that higher status groups tend to have a greater amount of social participation, both formal and informal, than lower status groups. The Lynds said it of Middletown thirty years ago, and almost twenty years ago Mather showed that higher income groups participate in organizations to a much greater extent than lower income groups.[19] And through the years, more elaborate but similar studies have tended to verify this basic observation.[20] And further, if these relatively high status groups continue their frequent participation in formal and informal associations when they become suburban residents, no one should be surprised.[21] But the impact of much of the writing on

---

[17] William H. Whyte, Jr., "The Outgoing Life," p. 156.

[18] Hal Burton, "Trouble in the Suburbs," p. 117.

[19] William G. Mather, "Income and Social Participation," pp. 380-383.

[20] See, for example, Mirra Komarovsky, "The Voluntary Associations of Urban Dwellers," pp. 686-698; Genevieve Knupfer, "Portrait of the Underdog," pp. 103-214; Floyd Dotson, "Patterns of Voluntary Association among Urban Working Class Families," pp. 687-693; Leonard Reissman, "Class, Leisure, and Social Participation," pp. 76-84; and the Bay area studies of Wendell Bell, for example, Wendell Bell and Maryanne T. Force, "Social Structure and Participation in Different Types of Formal Associations," pp. 345-350, and "Urban Neighborhood Types and Participation in Formal Associations," pp. 25-34.

[21] Walter Martin, on the other hand, tells us that "Commuters participate less than noncommuters in voluntary associations and informal groupings *in the residence community*" (emphasis supplied). See Martin, *op. cit.*, p. 448. There may be no conflict between Martin's statement and mine. For one thing, the "suburbs" studied by ecologists may have little in common with mass-produced tract sub-

the mass-produced suburbs such as Park Forest, Levittown, *et al.*, is to suggest that the hyperactive "frantic socializing" in them is not so much a function of the status of their residents, as of suburban residence itself. Participation is not explained by reference to the assumption that most residents are members of the new white-collar occupations, and presumably, therefore, prone to active social participation; the suburb itself, apparently, intensifies proneness to "join," to be sociable, and to be convivial. Now in the absence of any suburban studies which try to find out to what extent the participation of its residents is due to their social position and to what extent to the fact that they are suburbanites, our study may provide something of a substitute.[22] For if the suburb itself is conducive to social participation, its effects should be evident even in a sample of factory workers.

FORMAL PARTICIPATION

There is no evidence that participation in formal associations has increased since our respondents have moved to the suburb. Indeed, we find very little formal participation at all; 70 per cent of our respondents belong to no clubs, organizations, or associations at all; only 8 per cent belong to more than one. In addition, 20 per cent of our respondents belong to fewer organizations in the suburb than they did before the move—somewhat higher than the 17 per cent who belong to more organizations. The large majority, however, have not been affected one way or another. Cross tabulations of organization membership by age, job, education, rural-urban origin, and type of former residence reveal no sharp unambiguous tendencies; in no group under any of these

urbia—the developments about which Whyte, Henderson, Riesman, and I are speaking. The ecologist's suburb may be merely an urban fringe with a sprinkling of residential clusters. Martin says also that commuters participate in associations to a greater extent in communities *other than* the one in which they live—obviously, the city in which they work, and presumably because of lack of opportunity in the fringe area. On the other hand, the mass-produced suburbs provide plenty of opportunity.

[22] A good deal of emphasis in the literature is placed upon the fact that suburbanites make friends through their children with a consequent intensification of their social life. But it is difficult to see what is uniquely suburban about this phenomenon. Parents with small children are usually young, and people in their twenties and thirties generally have a more active social life than older people. In general, this is true of our sample, but there is nothing suburban about it.

TABLE 5.1

Men's Organizations and Number Belonging

Dad's Club (PTA)	9
Moose	8
Church Brotherhood	3
Masons	2
Eagles	2
Woodsmen	2
American Legion	2
Foresters	2
Scoutmaster	2
Other organizations[a]	11
Total	43

[a] With one member in each.

variables does the frequency of "no membership" fall under 63 per cent. It is true that the rural born and those less than 40 years old tend to have somewhat more memberships than those of urban origin and those more than 40. More surprising, however, is the fact that those with a high school education or more tend to have *fewest* memberships. But in none of these cross tabulations are the figures very striking. (See appendix table A.13.)

Tables 5.1 and 5.2 list the organizations to which our respondents belong and the number of times each was mentioned. Notice

TABLE 5.2

Wife's Organizations and Number Belonging

Mothers' Club (PTA)	20
Christian Women's Auxiliary	3
Girl Scouts	2
Cub Scout Dens	2
Sewing Club	2
"Secret Pals Club"	2
Other organizations[a]	6
Total	37

[a] With one member in each.

here that only nine fathers belong to the PTA, a far cry from the
"everybody" that Henderson says belongs to the PTA in suburbia.
Notice also that, with the exception of the Moose and the PTA,
no more than three respondents belong to the same organization—
and some of the Moose are merely maintaining their Richmond or
Oakland memberships, but actually are quite inactive. What this
general lack of common memberships means is that there is not
much formal contact among our respondents in organizations to
which they mutually belong. It is also interesting that the civic
improvement club and the garden club are local suburban groups
in which we would expect lively participation—especially in the
improvement club, to which, presumably, it would be to everyone's interest to belong. But over and above our one respondent
who belongs (and he is its president—a Ford foreman), only one
other of our respondents had even heard of its existence, and he
claimed that he was too busy to join. The only organizations mentioned in which the member was really active were the hobby
organizations; one respondent, with a pilot's license, spends a considerable part of his spare time at the San Jose airport. The ama-
teur astronomer and the square dance enthusiast also devote a
good part of their spare time to their avocations. But the members
of the fraternal organizations (Moose, Masons, Woodsmen, For-
esters, Eagles, Elks) and the veterans' organizations are characteristically inactive, and in some cases have not even bothered to
have their Richmond or Oakland memberships transferred to San
Jose.

Although the wives of the Ford workers, like their husbands,
tend to have few memberships in organizations, there has been,
for them, a noticeable increase in their memberships since the
move to the suburbs. Sixty-four per cent of the wives belonged to
no organizations at all, and only 4 per cent to more than one, but
25 per cent of the wives belong to more organizations in the suburb than they did previously, whereas only 5 per cent belong to
fewer organizations. As table 5.1 indicates, the PTA probably
accounts for the greatest part of the increase. Indeed, community
activities (such as those represented by PTA, Girl Scouts, Camp-
fire Girls, and the like) command most of whatever organizational
participation the women have time for. With the exception of one

couple, who belong to a kind of self-improvement club ("We make speeches and learn poise and how to make eye contact"), and the two young wives who have organized their "kaffee-klatsches" into a "Secret Pals Club," the community organizations are the only one which get what little active participation there is.

On the whole, participation in organizations, as measured by frequency of attendance at meetings, is meager for both the men and the women. Of the 30 men who reported belonging to one or more organizations, 2 never go to meetings, 11 go rarely, 9 occasionally, and 8 often. Of the 32 women who reported memberships in organizations, 12 attend meetings rarely, 9 occasionally, and 11 often. But whereas the figures for the women again represent an increase over the frequency of their former participation, the figures for the men represent a decrease. Twenty-six per cent of the men attended meetings less often in the suburb than they did previously; 19 per cent attended meetings more often. But these last mentioned figures were not distributed evenly over the sample. It was those more than 40 years old who contributed most heavily to the decrease in attendance at meetings. For both the 20- to 29-year-old group and the 30- to 39-year-old group, a greater percentage went to meetings more often in the suburb. Similar tendencies are evident in the absolute frequencies with which the men attend meetings; attendance at meetings drops sharply after age 40. Of the 17 men who reported going to meetings "occasionally" or "often," 12 were less than 40.

The memberships and activity of the wives seem to be related only to whether or not they are employed outside the home. Of the wives, 34 per cent had full-time, part-time, or seasonal (mostly in the canneries) jobs outside the home, but only 25 per cent of the employed women were members of organizations. With the same figures arranged another way, 23 per cent of the employed women belonged to one or more organizations, but 39 per cent of the women who do not have jobs outside the home belonged to one or more organizations.

But again, I do not want to emphasize the importance of these minor variations, since the size of the sample prevents attaching much significance to them. The major point is that organizational membership and activity seem not very pronounced among these suburbanites. Clearly, this is not because of the absence of any objective opportunity; there *is* a civic improvement club and there *are* hobby clubs, and, to be sure, there is a PTA. But 9 fathers and 20 mothers, although not low, are not terribly high figures for membership in an organization (PTA) which we have been led to believe commands the attention of all suburban parents. In sum, although the women are more active in organizations than before, and the men less active than before, we can say that these suburbanites do not "suffer from a surfeit of inclusions" in clubs, organizations, and associations.

These figures on membership and activity in formal organizations include neither membership in the union (to which all of our sample belong except the twelve foremen, the engineer, and the service station operator) nor in a church.[23] The figures on attendance at union meetings were consistently low, but nevertheless difficult to interpret. Of those belonging to the union, 27 per cent reported that they never attended meetings, 48 per cent attended rarely, 16 per cent occasionally, and 9 per cent often. These crude figures are the important ones, since (with the exception of the Republicans, noted in chapter iii) cross tabulations failed to reveal any marked variations for the subgroups in their patterns of attendance at union meetings. Part of the difficulty of interpreting these seemingly low figures is because they suggest in spite of themselves, an average meeting attendance somewhat higher than comparative figures might lead us to expect. Although attendance at local union meetings has only recently begun to be studied in any detail,[24] Sayles and Strauss have concluded that "Except for skilled locals in the needle trades and very small locals of less than

---

[23] Mather's statistics (*op. cit.*) on organizational affiliation *did* include church membership, and this accounted for most of the participation of his low income sample. Komarovsky and those following her, however, have *not* included church membership as an organization affiliation.

[24] As recently as twelve years ago C. Wright Mills could say, "There are no good studies on American unions as a whole, or on any number of individual unions, to tell us how many union members fall into the inactive, active, or leader categories." Mills goes on to say, "It is a generous guess to estimate that 15 per cent of union members . . . are continuously active." On the basis of the figures cited by Sayles and Strauss, Mills' estimate is more than generous; it is virtually philanthropic. See C. Wright Mills, *The New Men of Power*, p. 38. See also Leonard R. Sayles and George Strauss, *The Local Union: Its Place in the Industrial Plant*, especially the detailed table on p. 173.

200, attendance [at average union meetings] varies from 2 to 6 per cent [of the membership]." [25] The difficulty is compounded by the fact that in spite of the reports of the respondents regarding their attendance at meetings, the Milpitas Ford local had not had a meeting for almost a year before the opening of their new union hall and recreation center, simply because they could never get a quorum.[26] Since the new union hall has opened, however, attendance at meetings, according to one informant, has averaged between 7 and 10 per cent of the membership. Many of those who reported that they attend union meetings very infrequently cited as a reason the fact that the union did not have a union hall; others, apparently, have not given the matter much thought, for some seemed surprised when they realized, "Why, I haven't been to a meeting since we've been living down here." At this writing, of course, it is not possible to say whether the new union hall will have a lasting effect upon attendance at meetings. If their suburban status has not affected the normal rank and file apathy, then low attendance may continue. On the other hand, if recent attendance is an indication of what the future may hold, the facilities offered by the new union hall plus the fact that it is *right in* a suburban tract (and thus continuous with as well as contiguous to the rest of their suburban existence) may contribute to a continuing increase in participation in union affairs.

INFORMAL SOCIAL RELATIONS

The evidence regarding informal social participation is more difficult to interpret, and this may be owing to the limitations of our interviewing; without participant observation, the quality of informal social contacts is difficult to apprehend. This difficulty is evident in some of the statistical findings. For example, although 54 per cent of the sample claimed to have made many new friends since the move to the suburb, only 19 per cent reported being very friendly with their neighbors, who constitute the overwhelming majority of their new friends. Similarly, although 78 per cent of

---

[25] Sayles and Strauss, *op. cit.*, p. 173.

[26] The new union hall and community center, in a union-sponsored inter-racial housing tract near Milpitas, was completed some months after the interviews were completed.

the sample said that they entertain friends at home at least once a month, only 13 per cent reported that they visit their neighbors often. Again, although 38 per cent of the respondents reported that they entertain friends at home more often in the suburb than in their previous residence, 27 per cent reported that they entertain less often. Certainly, these are difficult data to interpret. There is, however, some form in the data. As a generalization, it seems fair to say that the *least* privileged subgroups in our sample manifest *most* increase in their informal social participation. This is *not* to say that their informal contacts are more frequent than those who come from more privileged backgrounds. Quite the contrary: the former homeowners, the better educated, and the foremen participate informally more often than the former renters, the poorly educated, and the workers, but the *increase* is greater for these latter groups than for the former.

For example, appendix table A.14 shows that the former homeowners entertain friends more often than does either group of renters, but appendix table A.15 shows that these former homeowners are the only ones of the three groups who had a net decrease in the amount of entertaining they do since the move to the suburb. Similarly, although the better educated entertain friends at home more often than the poorly educated, table A.15 shows that it is the best educated group whose *increase* is least in the amount of entertaining they do.[27] These data seem to suggest that suburban residence *by itself* does not lead to a significant increase in the amount of entertaining people do. Presumably, the homeowners, the well educated, and the men with high status jobs would have entertained more before the move; they still do more than the other groups do but apparently *not as much* more, and it seems reasonable to suppose that the marked increase in entertaining among the renters is simply due to the fact that they have more living room than they had previously—more room for guests —and to the pride they probably feel in having a pleasant home into which to invite people.

---

[27] Similarly, although the foremen entertain friends at home more often than the workers, they are the only job group which entertains less often in San Jose than they did previously.

Nevertheless, an index as crude as the frequency with which people "have others in" tells us nothing, really, about the quality of such contacts. For example, it does not tell us whether this "entertaining" refers to an evening of invited quests or whether it refers to a casual beer together with neighbors on a Saturday afternoon during a break from puttering with the engines of their automobiles. The fact that 38 per cent said they entertain about once a week and 40 per cent about once a month does not square with the fact that only 13 per cent say they visit their neighbors often and 59 per cent say rarely. It seems probable that most of this "entertaining" is not planned or "invited," but rather spontaneous and extremely casual. For one thing, most of the interviewing was done between 4:30 and 9:00 P.M., and it was a rare event for the interviews to be interrupted by a neighbor coming in or the telephone ringing. Also, in making appointments for the interviews, it was invariably suggested to me that virtually any night would be all right, at my convenience, so to speak, indicating that their evenings were almost always "free." In addition, driving through these tracts, I do not remember one occasion where the number of cars parked on the street indicated that someone was entertaining guests. What I did encounter frequently was a couple of neighbors looking under the hood of a troublesome car, or one offering advice to another on a do-it-yourself project at the door of the garage, or simply standing in their joint driveways watching the cool of the evening come on, and remarking upon it.

These, of course, are impressions; yet the impression that there is not much "entertaining" in the sense of invited visiting in this suburb is supported by the comments of some of the respondents themselves. One, explaining why, although he has made many new friends, he and his wife do not visit neighbors much, remarked, "not like we go to them to play bridge and they come here, but just friends." Still another said that "in Richmond there was always people to take care of the kids; here all are strangers." And yet another, indicating his acquaintance with the myth of suburbia, said, "we're not too much on socializing. It isn't that kind of neighborhood where they're running in all the time. We're a laboring class of people; we work for an hourly wage."

The accuracy of these testimonials is reflected by figures which show that the percentage of those who visit their friends often is extremely low. But the very notion of "friend" here is problematical. They report that they have made many new friends, and the vast majority of these new friends have been made through the neighborhood.[28] But precisely how "friendly" one must be with another in order for him to be thought of as a "friend" seems to be rather minimal. This is indicated not only by the substantial majority who visit their friends only rarely but by the fact that only 19 per cent said that they were "very" friendly with their two closest neighbors; on the other hand, 34 per cent reported that their relationship with their two closest neighbors was one of nodding acquaintance. When we look at the neighbors and friends of our respondents, we have a beginning of an explanation of the infrequent mutual visiting and the fact that more than one-third of our respondents say that they are barely on speaking terms with their two closest neighbors. Appendix table A.16 shows that a large majority of both their friends and neighbors are working-class people, whom we would normally expect to do little mutual visiting or otherwise engage in semistructured "sociable" behavior.

Floyd Dotson takes issue with Komarovsky and others who have suggested that the lack of formal memberships in associations and informal contact with friends among working-class people means that they are socially isolated and cut off from the channels of power, information, and growth. He argues that this analysis fails to take into consideration the strong familial ties: "The role of informal social participation, particularly within the family and kin group has, we believe, consistently been underestimated." Dotson is right about the family but there is still considerable doubt about the extent of informal participation among working-class *friends*. Notice in appendix table A.17 that 4.5 per cent of the occupations of the two closest friends of the respondents were unknown; in other words the occupations of nine people who were classified as "closest friends" were unknown to those whose closest friends they were. This is hardly closeness. One of my respondents

---

[28] The distinction between "neighbors" and "plant friends" is only partially valid since their neighbors are to a large extent fellow Ford workers.

admitted to me, "I don't think it pays to have a lot of friends—
maybe because we have so many relatives." [29] On the other hand,
consistent with the findings of other students, the data indicate
that our respondents do a considerable amount of vising with their
relatives. Whereas only 19 per cent visit their relatives rarely,
47 per cent visit them often. Only 4 per cent of our sample (a
sample, it should be remembered, with a history of great geo-
graphical mobility) had no relatives within easy visiting distance.

This finding suggests a rather interesting question which is
worth a brief digression: Is it true that working-class people who
are geographically (but not socially) mobile tend to move either
as an extended family unit or as a nuclear family unit to areas
where other members of the extended family have previously
moved, whereas the geographically *and* socially upward mobile
move only as isolated nuclear families to the place where corporate advancement beckons? If it were true, it would help explain a number of interesting facts apparently prevalent in white-
collar suburbs populated by upward mobile families. From various
descriptions of neighboring and other informal contacts in such
suburbs (the proverbial coming and going without knocking, the
easy familiarities and intimacies on relatively brief acquaintance,
and so on), it is apparent that friends serve as a kind of functional
equivalent of kin for isolated, upwardly mobile nuclear families
without immediately available relatives. They do for the isolated
nuclear family what kin have traditionally done: they provide
sympathy in time of sorrow, recognition for achievement, support
in time of need, gossip regarding the occupational rather than
the familial community, and togetherness at holiday seasons. The
importance of these functions may also help explain the strong
negative emotional attitudes of young upward mobiles toward
their parents' traditional warning that "blood is thicker than
water." There is probably no better way for the parental generation to provoke sullen, inarticulate rage in their children (flown far
from the coop) than to tell them that their fine friends, so loyal

---

[29] Floyd Dotson, *op. cit.*, p. 688; cf. Paul Lazarsfeld and Robert Merton,
"Friendship as Social Process," in Morroe Berger *et al.*, *Freedom and Control in
Modern Society*, in which they report that 10 per cent of their respondents did not
know as many as three persons whom they could properly describe as really close
friends. (See p. 21.)

and true, will desert them in time of need, but that their families will stand by them through thick and thin. Homilies like this can provoke so strong a response because the mobile, isolated nuclear family has a *vested interest* in proving that water may indeed be just as thick as blood.

To return to our data, the pattern of informal social participation manifested by our sample seems to be much as we would expect from a working-class population. Mutual visiting between friends and neighbors seems to be infrequent; on the other hand, participation in family activities seems to occur often. But very little of significance comes out of our cross tabulations for the figures on visiting. The most striking finding is that those more than 50 years old do very little visiting of any kind. The younger people, the well educated, the former home owners, and the foremen do slightly more visiting than comparable subgroups, but in no case are the figures very striking. An impression worth reporting is that those individuals who do seem prone to social activity tend to find their friends outside the plant-tract community—usually through the church. A few white-collar friends were made through the wife's job. Where wives work in an office, they meet other white-collar people who, presumably, do more entertaining than blue-collar people. One of the respondents' wives (who said they did a lot of entertaining and visiting) added, "but we don't associate with anybody from the plant." Another woman, a young college graduate and former social worker (married to a Ford worker who used to be a school teacher in Palestine), reported that, "This is a cold neighborhood but we have a much fuller and busier life than we had previously because of other friends we've met through the Unitarian church." [30]

Indeed, it seems to be precisely the women who, in the daytime, engage in most of what sociable behavior does go on. There does seem to be some validity in the image of female "kaffeeklatsching" in suburbia, and as a general impression it seems fair to report that the women seem much more "suburban" than the men do, that is to say, they more closely approximate the image of "the

---

[30] This woman, in response to the question asking for class identification, answered "lower middle class" with a look of utter and complete confidence that she was giving the correct answer.

suburbanite" than the men. For one thing, most of them are at home all day, which means simply that the impact of "suburban living" on them is greater than on the men, who spend the whole day, as they have always done, in the plant.[31] It was both interesting and amusing to watch the responses of husband and wife to the questions which had obvious class and status relevance. In at least two cases, to the question asking for class membership, the simultaneous response was "working class" from the husband and "middle class" from the wife; similarly, the wives seemed more prone to rate their present neighbors "higher class" than the husbands were. The women go to church more than the men do, and 62 per cent of the women report that they visit housewives in the neighborhood during the day "often" or "occasionally;" of the 32 per cent of the wives who visit other wives only rarely, most of them are women who work during the day. This daytime female "kaffeeklatsching" is interesting not so much for its own sake as for the response of the husbands to it. Apparently it is the cause for a lot of kidding; almost invariably, when I came to the question, the husbands would assume a pose of mock indignation (there is a distinct wife-kidding look that appears on men's faces; it mixes secret pride, envy, and affectionate disapproval of a spouse's "mischievous" doings),[32] suggesting, sometimes explicitly, that "all these women do is drink coffee and yak, yak, yak." I mention this only because the mock indignation suggests that this is something that they really should not do, or, at any rate, that they have not done in the past; it is *mock* indignation because the hus-

[31] In Richmond, more than half of the wives of the married men were employed, more than one-third of them *full time*. In the suburb, only slightly more than one-third are employed, and only 18 per cent full time. This reduction in the number of working wives is a mixed blessing. For some, of course, it means more time for homemaking and for "kaffeeklatsching" and other kinds of neighborly activity. For others, it means an enforced idleness and isolation which in some cases may be quite difficult to bear. Two of our respondents lost their wives simply because of an inability on their part to survive happily in the suburb; the wives simply picked up and went back to their jobs in Richmond. For one it has meant divorce; for the other, the divorce proceedings are pending, but may never go through because the family is nominally Catholic.

[32] Much like, ostensibly, the attitude of the peasant farmer toward his son who comes home to the family acres with a degree from the agricultural college: a mixture of pride and canny distrust of the ability of science to command the seasons; pride in accomplishment mixed with apprehension about the consequences of the accomplishment for the traditional ways of the father. Something like this is probably a constant in the relationship between generations in mobile societies.

bands do not *really* believe that there's anything reprehensible about it, but only that it isn't the sort of thing that the wives of factory workers usually do. And the "indignation" seems to be simply a variety of status envy that the wives can actually bring it off successfully, whereas their own (the men's) ability to "be sociable" is limited by their lack of time and necessary "social skills." This ability of the wives to be sociable is without doubt related to the fact that, on the whole, they are considerably better educated than their husbands. Twenty-six per cent of the men have a high school education or better; 40 per cent of the women have a high school education or better. Only 19 per cent of the women have an eighth-grade education or less; 39 per cent of the men have not gone beyond the eighth grade, I should add, of course, that there is a substantial minority of wives who do not bother with kaffeeklatsching, but even their explanations of why they don't, imply the existence of kaffeeklatsching as a dominant motif. "I don't visit other housewives much because they're cliquey and gossipy and tale-telling," said one woman; another put it more bluntly: "I'm not the coffee-crowd type."

What goes on at these kaffeeklatsches we cannot precisely say, but there seems to be considerable doubt that theories of child rearing occupy a prominent place. This is not to say that the women do not discuss their children; I mean only that the "baby bibles" probably do not have much place in their discussions. Forty-three per cent of the mothers admit having read nothing at all on child rearing. Of the majority who *did* claim to have read some things on child rearing, almost half could not remember the name or author of a single thing they had read. Thirty-three per cent of the mothers did, however, remember what they had read, but it is instructive that Spock is mentioned six times and Gesell twice. *Parents* magazine is the most widely read authority on child rearing.[33] Twenty-six per cent of the mothers say that they discuss with their friends the things they've read, but as often as not the conclusions reached are negative ones. "I don't go by the book. I go by the way my parents raised me." "I use a mother's instinct."

---

[33] Something called *Mother's Encyclopedia* was mentioned six times and insurance company pamphlets three times. These two, plus Spock, Gesell, and *Parents,* were the only literature on child rearing mentioned.

"I don't believe in those kind of books. Our own ideas are just as good." These statements, chosen from many others like them, represent not only the attitudes of those who do not read on child rearing but also, with a few exceptions, the responses of those who have read.

Although the women apparently do quite a bit of daytime mutual visiting, evening visiting between couples is, as I have suggested, rare except with kinsfolk; couples visit their relatives but not their friends. What else do they do with their spare time? Do they go to parties? Do they "go out" on week ends? If the women kaffeeklatsch do the men spend evenings "out with the boys"? Again, the answer is, on the whole not very much, but here age and education play an important role. For example, although more than half of the sample "go out" on week ends rarely or never, appendix table A.17 shows that it is the better educated people who account for most of whatever going out there is. Similarly, none of the respondents reported that they go to parties often, but 84 per cent reported that they go to parties never or rarely. Only 16 per cent report going to parties "sometimes," but appendix table A.18 shows that most of these are persons with a high school education or better. Appendix table A.18 is interesting also for the tendency it shows for partygoing to decrease as age increases. But again, I want to emphasize that these cross tabulations should not obscure the fact that partygoing and going out on weekends is a relatively rare occurrence for the sample as a whole. This is particularly true if we remember that much of this activity may be *family* activity. Much of the week-end going out entails trips back to Richmond to visit with family, and, ostensibly, some of these get-togethers would be classified in the respondents' minds as "parties." [34] As for the rest, week-end going out means mainly an occasional drive-in movie, an evening at the auto races, or a drink and some dancing at local taverns which have music on week ends. In addition, week-end going out has, on the whole, shown a net decrease since the move to the suburb; 32 per cent of the sample reported that they "go out" less often than they did

---

[34] Seventy-one per cent of the sample say that they still have some or many friends in Richmond, but 56 per cent say they see their Richmond friends rarely or never. They do make frequent trips to Richmond but probably spend most of their time there visiting with relatives.

previously, but 21 per cent go out more often. Nor do the men typically spend evenings "out with the boys"; 62 per cent say they never do and only 3 per cent say "often." Of those who do spend evenings out occasionally, it means the bowling alley or a few drinks with the boys after a union or club meeting.

OTHER FORMS OF LEISURE

To raise the question of formal and informal participation is to raise the question of what people do with their spare time. The burden of this chapter has been to show that, with the exception of family relationships and daytime, women's kaffeeklatsches, organizational participation and mutual visiting of a semiformal sort among friends and neighbors are slight. "Neighboring" of an extremely casual sort, and usually of short duration, is, as I have suggested, probably quite frequent; but the fact that people do not, apparently often invite each other to their homes suggests either that they have not yet mastered middle-class, sociable "know how" or that the home is still conceived in working-class terms, as a place for the family. But if most of them do not visit much and do not go out and do not invite people to their homes and do not go to parties, what is it that takes most of their leisure time?

Movies, we can say immediately, do not command much of their entertainment budget. Appendix table A.19, for example, shows that more than half of our respondents go to movies "never" or "rarely." It was no intellectual, but rather an American cracker-barrel type who said to me, "I wouldn't give you a nickel for any movie." The fact that the motion picture industry apparently fails to win the entertainment dollar of these factory workers may be a result not so much of the "threat of television," as of the fantasies of upward mobility portrayed on the screen, to which many so-called "escapist" films appeal. This is no gratuitous comment on "mass culture." When movie attendance is cross tabulated with education, as in appendix table A.19, we find that those with a high school education or more go to movies almost twice as often as those with an eighth-grade education or less. Similar figures, although not as unambiguous, appear when movie attendance is cross tabulated with age. These data suggest that youth and education, which are known to be related to mobility expectations, may also be related to the frequency with which one attends movies.[35] What I am suggesting here is that, given the content of many American films, it may be possible to consider moviegoing an index of aspiration. Although moviegoing has decreased sharply for the sample as a whole since the move to the suburb (39 per cent go less often; 19 per cent go more often), the decrease has been *least* for the best educated group. This cannot be blamed on television since almost all owned television sets before moving to the suburbs.

Further support for the notion that many working-class people fail to identify themselves with the images of mobility portrayed in the mass media can be found in their television preferences.[36] The question asking our respondents to list their favorite TV shows produced rather startling results because there seemed to be virtually no interest in what, at the time of the interviews, were the most heavily publicized and highest rated shows. Steve Allen's show, for example, was mentioned once, Perry Como's twice, Ed Sullivan's three times, and that domestic comedy show, supposedly beloved by all Americans, "I Love Lucy," was mentioned twice. "The $64,000 Question" fared somewhat better, being mentioned six times, but the prize fights were mentioned 38 times and the "western" show, "Cheyenne," was mentioned 37 times.[37] Table 5.3 lists the preferred television shows by type, and the number of times they were mentioned. This list can bear some close scrutiny. Notice the wide gap between the westerns and the sports shows on the one hand, and the rest of the preferences on the other. Apparently the only TV shows which command the attention of a majority of the group are the westerns and the sports events, that is, those shows largely without middle-class content.

---

[35] It is well known, for example, that young people constitute a very high percentage of the movie audience, that is, people among whom mobility expectations are presumably still relatively high. Younger people are also likely to be better educated than older people. Thirty-nine per cent of our sample had an eighth grade education or less but nobody less than 30 fell into this group.

[36] Everyone interviewed owned at least one television set. A few owned two, and mentioned this fact with some pride.

[37] In the interval since the interviews were completed, westerns have glutted the television air, and are presently still very highly rated. At the time of the interviews, however, westerns had not nearly the national popularity they attained in subsequent months.

TABLE 5.3

Type of TV Show and Number of Times Mentioned

Westerns	68
Sports events	64
Adventure	29
Comedy	22
Quiz	20
Variety	18
Mystery	14
Serious drama	6

Indeed westerns are often characterized by a satiric or otherwise contemptuous treatment of respectable, middle-class townsfolk. In brief, these people seem to care very little about what I think it is fair to call "middle-class" entertainment. Even their taste for comedy runs not to the stereotyped domestic situations characteristic of "I Love Lucy" or "Father Knows Best" but to the rough and tumble comedy of Sergeant Bilko, McGraw, and Groucho Marx—who, like most other great American comedians, has done little else for the last thirty years but satirize the middle class. I remember being struck one evening when, upon entering a home for an interview, I encountered my prospective respondent sitting expressionless on the couch in his blue-jean overalls, stained with grease and grime, watching as a smooth-cheeked announcer demonstrated the virtues of a new-type deodorant on the screen of the TV set. To whom was he speaking? I asked myself; he was not speaking to that man on the couch. On the other hand, I remember walking in for another interview while a western was on the TV screen and was struck by the fact that the accent of the actor had the same southwestern drawl as the speech of my respondent.

Television, however, does give us the answer to what they do with most of their spare time: they watch television. Appendix table A.20 summarized the number of hours per week that they spend in front of the television set. If, as the table indicates, almost half of the sample spends more than 16 hours a week watching television, then this accounts for a goodly part of their leisure time. Cross tabulating age and education with time spent in front of the television set revealed no clear trends. Indeed, the very failure of so many of our cross tabulations to turn up unambiguous trends suggests that the most important variable may be the one we are holding constant: the fact that these are factory workers.

There remains one more point to cover, namely the quality of home life. Does the fact that our respondents spend a lot of time at home mean that they devote a lot of time *to* their home? Is their taste improving? Are they taking on such gracious habits as wine with dinner or a cocktail before it? *Fortune*'s article on the suburban market, for example, has told us that "Suburbia's taste . . . is also growing better. . . . Almost everywhere esthetics rears its handsome head. Suburbia has a good eye for color, and it keeps abreast of the latest developments in the art of living, at least as that art is set forth in the many women's and home magazines." [38] First, we can say that the residents of the suburb under discussion certainly do subscribe to magazines, not only to the "women's and home" magazines but to numbers of others as well. Table 5.4 lists by name and type all the magazines mentioned more than once to which our respondents reported having subscriptions. In addition to the striking prevalence of *Reader's Digest*,[39] we observe immediately that, given the fact that they *read* these magazines, they *are* exposed, as *Fortune* puts it, to "the latest developments in the art of living." It is also true that there has been about a 25 per cent increase in the number of their magazine subscriptions since the move to the suburb, and this increase is particularly strong in "women's and home" magazines. But how effective have these magazines been in placing a viable life style before the eyes of these readers? Do the subscriptions to these magazines represent an *interest* in the life style that dominates their pages? The impressions garnered from a survey of the furnishing style of the livingrooms leads one to doubt the success of the "women's and home" magazines in providing a viable model. The living rooms tend to be crowded with the overstuffed furniture that often appears in full page newspaper ads announc-

[38] "The Lush New Suburban Market," *Fortune* (November, 1953), p. 230.
[39] *Reader's Digest*, of course, is the most widely circulated magazine in the United States, but for 31 per cent of our sample to have subscriptions to it is a fantastically high figure, one for which we cannot account. The persistence of door-to-door salesmen in the suburbs may have something to do with it (see below), and, of course, there seems to be an elective affinity between the style of life of our respondents and that of *Reader's Digest*.

TABLE 5.4

MAGAZINE SUBSCRIPTIONS

Magazines	Number of Subscriptions
General interest	
Reader's Digest	31
Life	16
Saturday Evening Post	9
Look	8
Coronet	3
Colliers	2
Time	2
"Home" magazines	
Sunset	6
American Home	5
Better Homes and Gardens	5
Household	4
Women's magazines	
Good Housekeeping	8
Ladies' Home Journal	8
McCall's	4
Redbook	3
Men's magazines	
True	6
Popular Mechanics	3
Field and Stream	2
Argosy	2
Mechanix Illustrated	2
Miscellaneous	
Parents	11
True Story	5
St. Anthony's Messenger (Church)	5
Modern Romances	3
Children's Digest	2
Photoplay	2
Modern Screen	2

ing "three rooms of furniture for $199—no down payment." The mantle tends to become a glass or plaster menagerie. On the walls are not Renoir reproductions but F. W. Woolworth landscapes covered by glass, or else gilt-framed photographs of members of the family. The deviants, that is, those with "good taste," tend toward chintz and colonial maple. Why, then, the apparent lack of effect by these magazines? Many of these magazine subscriptions are probably due to the solicitations of door-to-door salesmen. Just as newlyweds are besieged by life insurance salesmen (who keep their eyes on marriage license records at the County courthouse), new suburbanites are assaulted by door-to-door salesmen, who assume that a family that moves into a new house needs everything: garden supplies, lawn mowers, major and minor appliances, vacuum cleaners, brushes, pictures of the baby, storm windows, encyclopedias, and magazines too. Now it may be a relatively easy task for some housewives to "get rid of" a salesman, but I doubt whether working-class housewives have much experience at this sort of thing; a salesman's time is valuable, and he probably would not devote much of it to canvassing a working-class neighborhood, if his net return is likely to be lower than in a middle-class neighborhood. In addition to the lack of "know-how" for getting rid of salesmen, it is possible that an element of flattery is initially experienced by working-class housewives to whom all these suave young men who ring the doorbell devote attention. But that these suburbanites have been burned by the devious ingenuities of the American salesman is evidenced by the amount of assurance I frequently had to devote to convincing my respondents that I was not a salesman, had nothing to sell, no pitch to make, and by the fantastic stories I was told of the cajoleries and subterfuges of salesmen who present themselves at the door as anything but what they are,[40] and by the frequently bitter assertions that they would not renew their magazine subscriptions, once they ran out.

The *Fortune* article on the suburban market goes on to say that "wine with dinner, for instance, is now uniformly regarded as a

---

[40] An encyclopedia salesman is an "educator" and the baby picture salesman comes from the "institute of photographic representation." These kinds of selling jobs are often filled by teachers, in order to supplement their incomes; consequently, the academic posture is easy to assume.

'nice thing,' and the local liquor store now sells so much table wine that it has had to add a large wine cellar. And in many new [suburban] communities there is a strong undercurrent of yearning for 'culture.' " [41] To our sample, wine with dinner is not conceived as a "nice" middle-class habit; wine with dinner is a "Dago" habit —something that goes with spaghetti, ravioli, and lasagna. More than three-quarters of the sample say they never have wine with dinner. Of the others, some will have wine with an occasional Italian dinner in a restaurant and eight respondents reported that they sometimes serve red wine when they have "company" for dinner. Beer, however, is not a beverage that goes with food; one has a beer after coming home from work or on weekend summer afternoons. Beer is the "cocktail" that comes before dinner. One middle-aged foreman and his office-manager wife reported that they generally have a martini before dinner. Seventy-six per cent reported that they never have a cocktail before dinner, and several of these responded as if they were not quite sure what the word meant. Of the 12 per cent who reported that they did have a cocktail before dinner occasionally, at least half meant that they had a shot of whiskey. Drinking in general seems to be quite moderate in the suburb. Twenty-nine per cent say their drinking has decreased since the move to the suburb; only 4 per cent report some increase in their drinking, and 13 per cent, mostly the Baptists, are teetotalers.

The quality of home life, then, seems to reflect few of the images of suburban life offered in the mass media. Nevertheless, this should not be interpreted invidiously; it would be a mistake to take the "failure" of this group to develop the stereotyped "suburban style" simply as evidence of its inability to transform material improvements in their standard of living into cultural improvements. It is possible that the vast improvements in material standard of living for workers represented by their trek to suburbia (*without,* it should be emphasized, the *social* mobility represented by white-collar status and a college degree) may provide the conditions for the development of a cultural style which, though not that of the suburban middle class, is not that of the urban working class of the past either.

⁴¹ "The Lush New Suburban Market," *op. cit.,* p. 234.

Chapter VI

Class Consciousness

It should be clear by now that in spite of the fact that the great majority of our respondents feel that their lives have been distinctly improved as a result of the move to the suburbs, it would be misleading to characterize this sense of being "better off" as an instance of individual status mobility, actual or incipient. For the most part, we have found few marked changes in behavior or belief since the move from Richmond, and none that can with complacency be attributed to the fact of suburban residence. We have seen that, on the whole, their aspirations are sharply limited, they do not participate much in organizations, they are still very much Democratic, they do not rely on child development experts, and so forth. At the same time, it would be difficult to overestimate the intensity with which they feel that they are "better off." They are homeowners in a bright new world of lawns, patios, electrical appliances, and pastel bathroom fixtures, and they have neighbors who, frequently, are experiencing the same exhilaration of arrival as they themselves. But what kind of "arrival" is this? How, for example, do they rank themselves and their neighbors on a stratificational scale? Does their distinct sense of being "better off" manifest itself in "middle-class" self-identifications? On the whole, we would say "no" but the answers are not unambiguous.

Although the results fluctuate somewhat, around half of the sample identified themselves as "working class" both before and after the move to the suburbs.[1] Appendix table A.21 shows only a slight upward shift in the self-rankings of our respondents since they have moved to the suburbs; approximately 5 per cent see themselves as moving into the middle class as a result of the move. There is only one marked difference between the figures reported in appendix table A.21 and those reported in appendix table A.22, which represents our respondents' ranking of their neighbors both before and after the move to the suburbs; 12 per cent of our respondents ranked their Richmond neighbors as *lower* class, and this fact is reflected in the relatively low percentage of those who ranked their Richmond neighbors as middle class. This difference, however, disappears in the rankings of their suburban neighbors, which are essentially the same as their self-rankings.

Nevertheless, these relatively small percentage differences do not square with the fact that 25 per cent of our respondents reported that they felt their suburban neighbors were "higher class" than their former neighbors. But this gross figure of 25 per cent varies enormously when cross tabulated by type of former residence. A look at appendix table A.23 shows that 23 per cent of the former renters of government apartments ranked their neighbors as "lower class"[2] but only 15 per cent ranked their neighbors as "middle class." What is important about this result is that it suggests that much of the upward mobility implied by the 25 per cent who reported their present neighbors as "higher" class than their former neighbors, is mobility *from lower class to working class*—although, to be sure, some of it is from working class to middle class. The probability of this suggestion is increased by the figures in appendix table A.24, which show that almost 70 per cent of those who ranked their present neighbors as "higher class" are former renters of government apartments.

---

[1] It should be emphasized again that the self-rankings and the rankings of others before the move are retrospective rankings. Similarly, the comparative rankings of present neighbors with former neighbors also involve a retrospective factor.

[2] In working-class lexicon, the term "lower class" is reserved for people who are not quite respectable. In the view of 23 per cent of the former residents of the government housing projects, their neighbors were predominantly lower class because "they were always fighting and running around" or "because they all used to be drunkards, like I used to be." One worker who still identified his suburban neighbors as working class in spite of the fact that they were much better off than they were in Richmond, commented, "In Richmond, they were *strictly* working class; some were lucky to be working" (emphasis in original).

We should note also that of the thirteen persons who ranked their present neighbors as "lower class" than their former neighbors, all were former homeowners; some of them had probably lived in neighborhoods that contained many middle-class people, and may have felt "down-graded" because of the predominantly working-class character of the suburb. But none of this should obscure the gross fact that 68 per cent of the respondents reported that their present neighbors were "about the same" class as their former neighbors. It is true that some respondents, although clinging to the view that their neighbors were the same class as their former neighbors, at the same time reaffirmed their sense of being "better off" and living among "nicer people." But this makes perfect sense; one can improve one's standard of living without this improvement constituting, or being perceived as, a step upward in the class hierarchy.

At the same time, these people are virtually all homeowners, and not only homeowners but suburban homeowners whose small castles look like the pictures in *House and Garden,* and this fact creates considerable ambiguity. One foreman, who reported that the class of his Richmond neighbors and that of his San Jose neighbors was about the same, went on to explain, "But the *environment* is different;[3] they *think* they're better off." Another respondent explained: "They [his suburban neighbors] are and they aren't working class because of their homes and because they have a goal in life. They are better people than they were in the government housing, but they're the same *class* of people; give a man opportunity and he'll be OK; keep him beat down and he'll be a bum." What these respondents (and others who spoke in the same vein) are clearly getting at is that although their incomes and their way of life remain largely unchanged, the fact of owning a new home in a community of new homeowners makes them more respectable and self-respecting people, "but they're the same *class* of people." As one recently arrived Polish immigrant eloquently put it, "My place is mine; rent is rent; is different."

Precisely what, however, do the class designations that were chosen mean? The designation "working class" is least ambiguous.

---

[3] The terms "environment" and "surroundings" were the ones most commonly used by the respondents to denote social and cultural influences.

Probes of the meaning of this term revealed an almost unanimous opinion that a member of the working class was someone who worked with his hands (or, as one man put it, "with his hands or his feet") for an hourly wage, and usually in a factory. One foreman, who identified himself as "on the fringe of the middle class," did so on the basis that the working class was characterized by manual labor; since he did not *quite* do manual labor, he belonged to the fringe of the middle class. "We're all working class around here," said one skilled worker; "I'm working class, a fellow who has to work with his hands." One foreman was more abrupt: "Working class is not being in business for yourself or not an executive. Truck drivers, cops, and Ford workers are working class." Being an "executive" apparently means earning a salary rather than an hourly wage, that is to say, having a "position." One respondent who identified middle-class people as those who are in business for themselves, qualified this when it was pointed out to him that the plant manager was not "in business for himself," by saying, "Well, he has a *position*." "We're working class," said another, "I work in a factory. Salaried people and people who own their own businesses are middle class." Or, "We're a laboring class of people; we work for an hourly wage; no executives around here." Or, "Middle class is on up in the executive class—the ones who always drive new cars."

Of course, the respondents who spoke like this constituted the bare majority or near majority who identified themselves and their neighbors as "working class." Although the largest single group of respondents preferred this designation, large enough minorities preferred to designate themselves and their neighbors as "middle class" (or by other middle-class labels) to be worth some analysis. More than one-third of the sample designated themselves and their suburban neighbors as "middle-class" people, and an additional 9 per cent chose to call themselves "average" or "medium" class people. But the bases of these various middle-class identifications are ambiguous; indeed, the manner in which those who identified themselves as middle class did so, ranged from a kind of hesitant or tentatively hopeful identification (a somewhat defensive, "Well, yeah, I guess we're middle class"—implying that there *was* some evidence in their suburban context to support such an identification) to the revealingly paradoxical comment of one man that, "around here, the working class *is* the middle class." Another unskilled worker, although identifying himself as "working class," qualified it with the statement that most of his neighbors were "good respectable people *who could pass for anything*" (emphasis supplied). Ostensibly, they can "pass for anything" because, as still another respondent remarked, "people around here seem to have more pride; they keep their things in better shape." This increased "pride" or "respectability" which for some is the source of their self-identification as "middle class," is clearly a function of owning a new suburban home in a community of peers. To be sure, pride of homeownership certainly might be thought of as evidence of heightened status consciousness; yet even here there is an ambiguity. Most of the respondents apparently do *not* think of their homes primarily as status objects. When asked about their reasons for preferring owning to renting (97 per cent preferred owning to renting; the rest had mixed feelings), the most frequent answers given were: (1) making payments on a home is an "investment"; the rent one paid produced only "rent receipts" whereas payments on a home mean "equity"; (2) it was cheaper to own than to rent; the payments they are making are not nearly what rent would be for comparable living quarters. Also mentioned frequently was the freedom to do as one pleased in one's own home, and the "privacy" that went with owning, that is, not being responsible to a landlord.[4] In addition, these men are handy, and many reported getting much pleasure out of working on and improving their property—again with a financial motive buttressing the "joy-in-work" motive. Relatively far down the list of reasons cited for preferring owning to renting are those having to do explicitly with status, for example, because "you met nicer people" or because "you lived in a nicer environment" or because "the kids have more opportunity here" or because "you feel it's your own and this makes you feel responsible." Although these overt manifestations of heightened status-consciousness occurred rela-

---

[4] It is worth noting here that the frequent emphasis on privacy as a desirable consequence of owning a tract home runs sharply counter to the comments of most students of white-collar suburbs, who often cite lack of privacy as one of the more ominous aspects of suburban living—ominous because it is an element of the problem of conformity.

tively infrequently, they occurred often enough to register an impression. It is perhaps best to put the matter this way: the largest group of respondents still classify themselves as "working class" in spite of the fact that they are conscious of a marked improvement in their standard of living. They can do this because their conception of what it means to be a member of the working class is clearly formulated in occupational terms. On the other hand, almost as large a group prefer to identify themselves as "middle," "average," or "medium" class.[5] Despite the fact that status pride in homeownership was not extremely pronounced, we can safely say that a small percentage of the sample rests its claim to membership in the middle class on the fact that they are "responsible," "respectable" homeowners. But, as we might infer from the relatively heavy emphasis on the financial meaning of homeownership (it's cheaper to own than to rent; owning is an investment, etc.), a somewhat larger percentage rests its claim to membership in the middle class solely upon income. Probing for the bases of middle-class self-rankings revealed that claims to membership in the middle class often rested upon the fact of making more than $4,000 per year; between $4,000 and $7,000 per year was, in the view of those who spoke in terms of dollars, a middle-class income. More than $7,500 per year really put one "up there," and less than $4,000 per year put one in the "lower class."

The $4,000 or $5,000 a year that these suburbanites make permit some of them to call themselves "middle class," but the framework or hierarchy of class which is meaningful to these workers is not a conceptual framework that applies to society as a whole, but one that is limited rather to *what is possible for them.* The income classes referred to above, though apparently having reference to society as a whole, lump together as "way up there" everyone who makes more than $7,000 or $7,500 per year; logically enough, this figure of $7,000 or $7,500 is the upper limit of what is possible for them; that is, a foreman can reasonably expect to reach this income figure eventually. To be "middle class," then, probably

---

[5] The vast majority of this group identified themselves similarly while they were still resident in Richmond, so that we can infer that residence in the new suburb does not directly act upon changes in class consciousness.

means to them, not what sociologists mean by middle class, but rather *middle of the working class.*

It should be stated immediately, of course, that this reference group hypothesis regarding class consciousness is only an interpretation, and cannot be conclusively proved with the available data. Still, the notion is far from unfamiliar, and there is both logic and evidence that can be submitted in at least partial support of it. One of the conclusions that Leonard Reissman drew from his study of levels of aspiration and social class was that:

The reference groups used by individuals appear to affect the relationship between class and aspirations. . . . The importance of the reference group appeared most clearly in the case of the policemen studied. . . . The policemen ranked low in the social class indices and low in aspiration levels. However, in a comparison with their own brothers, it became clear that they have made significant advances in occupational prestige. It can be argued that the brothers constituted the crucial reference group for the policemen and consequently, that their low level of aspiration is basically an expression of satisfaction with their present position. . . . In other words, they are now interested in settling down after having achieved success as measured in their terms.[6]

Reissmann, of course, was not speaking primarily of class consciousness, but it is not a great step from limiting one's aspirations in terms of what it is reasonable to suppose is possible to achieve, to limiting one's stratificational perspective, or class consciousness, to a *range of positions* which seem possible to achieve. In chapter ii, for example, I spoke of the highly refined criteria for "getting ahead" with which these automobile workers operate; if they perceive, say, a move from an assembly line job to a job as fork lift operator as a "promotion," as "getting ahead" (which they apparently do) then it means that they have a narrowly circumscribed stratificational framework, and if conceptions of mobility are formulated within this framework, a hierarchy of positions is also implied. From time to time, Eli Chinoy, in his otherwise very good book, recognizes this point, but he tends to slight its significance. He sees that automobile workers' "aspirations are controlled by a relatively objective appraisal of what is possible rather than by the unreliable image of America projected by the tradition of

---

[6] Leonard Reissman, "Levels of Aspiration and Social Class," pp. 241-242.

opportunity," but he interprets this in psychological terms as essentially rationalization of and defense against the guilt and self-blame generated by their failure to rise above the level of wage labor. In Chinoy's view, their redefinition of mobility, their projection of their hopes and aspirations onto their children, their emphasis on security (rather than mobility) and on the accumulation of possessions, are ultimately powerless against the psychologically "destructive character of guilt and self-blame." Chinoy concludes: "Both self-blame and defensive rationalizations against self-blame, however, contribute to the maintenance of both existing economic institutions and the tradition of opportunity itself. . . . American society escapes the consequences of its own contradictions. . . . The social order is thus protected, however, only at the psychological expense of those who have failed." [7]

But redefining the terms of advancement seems to me to be the first step in unhinging the escape hatch from Chinoy's psychological trap. Aspirations, mobility, and class consciousness are inherently relative conceptions; they imply a range of possibility, a range which, for the individual, changes throughout his life as he compares himself with different groups with which he deems himself comparable. In this connection, Goldschmidt says, "Concern over social position must always be seen in a matrix of social interaction; we always have status vis-à-vis real or imagined people. The community is only one possible context in which social status is seen, and probably for modern America not the most important. Professional people tend to view their social position in the context of their professional associates, and to some extent this is probably true of other occupation groups." [8] So far so good, but Goldschmidt is in error, I think, when he goes on to say, "The fundamental dynamic [of status] . . . lies in the assumption that 'you, too, can become president.' Behind this phrase stands the assumption not that we can or will enter the White House but that we can and will determine the level of our own status. . . . The 'rags to riches' theme enters every phase of our popular literature; our high school texts are filled with accounts of the careers

[7] Eli Chinoy, *Automobile Workers and the American Dream*, pp. 124-130.
[8] Walter Goldschmidt, "Social Class and the Dynamics of Status in America," p. 1211.

of Fords and Carnegies. . . ." [9] Goldschmidt is here forgetting
how little our high school texts affect us, and how "Horatio Alger"
and "rags to riches" are phrases which can no longer be uttered
with a straight face; their usage is now almost exclusively ironic
or derisive. Many workers are in this respect fully as sophisticated
as many social scientists who never tire of telling us that Horatio
Alger and rags to riches are myths. It is only children whose func-
tioning stratificational perspective includes a whole society; it is
only they who find it difficult to choose between being a cowboy
and being president.

The process of redefining the range of possibility among automobile workers seems to be only a special case of the process of
redefining ranges of possibility that go on among all occupational
strata. But this process is not an infinite one; although it is true
that levels of aspiration are continually reformulated in terms of
current level of achievement, there is a point below which rational
men know they are not likely to fall, just as there is a point above
which they know they are not likely to rise, and it is at this latter
point that some sort of final fulfillment must be experienced if the
psychological frustrations which torture people whose aspirations
are too high for possible achivement are not to occur. Under
such conditions, it is extraordinarily difficult, especially when one
is sympathetic with the interests of the working class, to remain
free from the kind of bias Chinoy reveals when he says, ". . . men
cannot spend eight hours per day, forty hours each week, in activity which lacks all but instrumental meaning." [10] For in the absence of evidence to the contrary (indeed, in light of the overwhelming evidence that they can and do), statements like this
reveal only that wage labor at the factory level seems terribly
unrewarding to Chinoy, and that he has sympathy for those who
seem to be alienated from meaningful work.

Whether or not the automobile worker suburbanites presently
under discussion are alienated from work is not at issue here.
What is, is their adjustment to certain circumscribed limits of possibility, and consequently, aspiration, circumscriptions which, as
I have suggested, are imposed not only on factory workers but to

[9] *Ibid.*, p. 1214.
[10] Chinoy, *op. cit.*, p. 130.

some extent on all occupational strata. In the case of the Ford workers, the upper limit of the aspirational framework is apparently foreman[11] or at best small business (usually a service station, a cafe, or a motel), and the lowest rung migrant farm labor or unemployment. Thus, in their own context, that of the plant and the suburb, they *are* middle class in a certain sense. That is, they are wealthier and live more comfortably than either their parents or most industrial workers of comparable social background; on the other hand, most of them are not quite as well off as, say, carpenters, electricians, printers, or service station operators. The suburb in which they live probably constitutes a fairly good sample of their range of possibility—from unskilled labor, to foremen and very small businessmen, with a few lower white-collar workers (postmen, bank tellers, supermarket checkers, and the like) thrown in. This reference group (the suburb and the occupational and income groups it represents) apparently constitutes the standard in terms of which not only aspirations but also consciousness of class are formulated. But the "upper" middle class, white-collar worlds of engineers, junior executives, professionals, and would-be professionals are completely beyond their ken; this latter milieu is alien to them, beyond their limits of possibility.

If this analysis is correct, then what being middle class means to these people is that they have achieved most of what they feel they have a right to expect out of life. Promotion to foreman will perhaps get them out of debt and provide a little extra money, but it will not substantially change their style of life. *Within* the reference group, of course, further distinctions will be observed. The man with the "good" job in the plant will be envied, the foreman will be viewed ambivalently, but his *status* within the group is clear. The service station owner is the local "prince"; he has realized a dream. But in large scale terms of status, their style of life constitutes them a single stratum. They have "arrived," and they can call themselves "middle class" because our society sanctions

---

[11] This does not apply so clearly to those who are already foremen. Of the 12 foremen included in the sample, 5 reported that they did expect to become managers or executives—almost one-half of the total number who reported that they did expect to become managers or executives. This fact, however, does tend to confirm the idea that levels of aspiration are reformulated in terms of current level of achievement.

the use of this term as a synonym for "comfortable," or "home-owner," or "a decent standard of living."

At the same time, this propensity to call oneself middle class is not evenly distributed throughout the sample. Those who were homeowners before moving to the suburb, the better educated, the young, the foremen, and the skilled workers show a greater propensity to designate themselves as middle class than the poorly educated workers, the older workers, the unskilled workers, and those who are owning homes for the first time in the suburb (see appendix tables A.25 and A.26). Similarly, the same groups with the greatest propensity to call themselves middle class are the groups who show least identification with the labor movement; that is, the younger workers, the better-educated workers, and the foremen, tend to believe more strongly than the other groups that organized labor has more power than it should have.[12] (See appendix table A.27.)

On the whole, however, the sample is quite conscious of the economic homogeneity of the suburb in which they live. Seventy-five per cent of the respondents reported that their neighbors were no better or worse off financially than they themselves; as many said, "We're all in the same boat here." But that boat is clearly not the same sleek craft to which William Whyte's Park Forest respondents continually referred.

---

[12] We should add here that the interviews were conducted at the height of the negative publicity regarding Dave Beck and the Teamsters Union.

Chapter VII

Conclusion

The study reported here is in a sense an attempt to test, on a working-class population, the validity of some of the influences that have been attributed to residence in new tract suburbs. The burden of the study has been to call into question certain commonly accepted facts of life in "suburbia," as these facts have been presented to us both by popular writers and by some professional social scientists. Although none of our findings gives us the right to doubt the truth of what many people have said of places like Park Forest and Levittown, they do give us permission to question the right of others to generalize about "suburbia" on the basis of empirical studies of selected samples whose "representativeness" has yet to be demonstrated. In other words, there are good reasons for believing that organization men live as Whyte says they do, and that the "new" middle class lives as others have said *they* do. But there is no reason to believe that what is characteristic of organization men or of the "new" middle class is also characteristic of the mass-produced suburbs. In a way, it is remarkable that, in spite of the efflorescence of the mass-produced suburbs in post–World War II America, references to "suburbia" more often than not cite the examples of Park Forest and Levittown—as if these two communities could represent a nation-wide phenomenon that has occurred at all but the lowest income levels and among most occupational strata.[1] At the same time, it would be arrogant to claim too much representativeness for the sample we have studied here. Auto workers are among the best paid of semiskilled manual workers; our tract is probably somewhat more homogeneous than most because of the circumstances of its occupancy; and, of course, the sample contains a heavy proportion of "Okies" and "Arkies."

It is true that some of our findings may seem to provide grounds for asserting that some social mobility has taken place among the group of suburbanites we studied. They claim, for example, many new friends, an increased interest in politics, and a new feeling of respectability. In addition, the milieu of the women in some ways approximates the female worlds reported as characteristic of white-collar suburbs. But it is important to keep in mind that the correlates of class are always temporary, and that not all correlates of class are equally important to membership in a class. Few people, that is, are mobile in *every* respect, and it is precisely in those respects *least* crucially associated today with the passage into a "suburban" milieu that changes can be noted in our sample. Home-ownership in a homogeneous community and high school education can adequately account for just about all the changes we have seen; but whereas at one time, to be a high school educated home-owner constituted important qualifications for membership in the middle class, today they qualify one only for "respectability."

On the other hand, it is precisely in those respects which, from the point of view of status stratification, are most crucial for entrance into a "suburban" milieu that we fail to discern changes in the style of life of the sample we studied. Membership and activity in formal associations are rare; so is semiformal mutual visiting between couples. There is little evidence of pronounced striving, status anxiety, or orientations to the future. They neither give parties nor go to them. Their tastes and preferences seem untouched by the images of "suburbia" portrayed in the mass media.

Although the major point I have tried to make here is that these

---

[1] Why have Park Forest and Levittown been studied and commented on *so much*? Is it only because Chicago and New York are centers of research personnel and facilities? Is it because Chicago and New York are centers of the mass media? Is the myth of suburbia one more example of the identification of "New York culture" with American culture? These are questions worth pursuing.

suburbanites have not, to any marked extent, taken on the patterns of behavior and belief associated with white-collar suburbs, I have also tried to emphasize their new feeling of well-being; they count; they feel like respectable people with a stake in the life of the community. "In Richmond," one respondent said, "we were one of the masses; down here there's community living." Adding this to the suggestion by Kornhauser and his colleagues that the working class can experience vast economic gains without necessarily losing their working-class orientations,[2] it is possible to envision a well-housed and domestically comfortable working class, conscious of their hard won material gains, aware of their concomitant position as responsible, respectable persons, and willing to act to see to it that these gains are not threatened by the unpredictable fluctuations of the economy.

But these "gains" are collective gains, and as such, they do not so much constitute evidence of individual social mobility as they do of the mobility of an entire stratum. In a prosperous society there occurs not only individual mobility between strata in a relatively stable hierarchy; the entire hierarchy is pushed upward by prolonged widespread prosperity, and is rearranged by changes in occupational or income distribution. At the same time, the function of stratification symbols is to maintain viable distinctions among different categories of people, and when criteria which formerly distinguished rank no longer do so because they have become widely available, it is not too much to expect a restructuring of the symbolic aspects of stratification—if, that is, their distinction-maintaining function is to remain viable.

It is perhaps for this reason that in recent years many students of stratification have deëmphasized the economic criteria of stratification in favor of the distinctly *social* criteria—that is, those having to do with style of life. For in a society in which even a semiskilled factory worker can earn $5,000 a year, own two cars, a ranch house, a TV set, and clothe his wife in excellent copies of Paris fashions the same year they are designed, it should perhaps be no surprise that higher status groups (perhaps without considerably greater income) should defend the potential threat posed by widespread material abundance to their "status-honor"

---

[2] Arthur Kornhauser, *et al.*, *When Labor Votes*, pp. 281-282.

by designating such economic possessions "vulgar" and asserting the indispensability of a particular style of life—that is, something that cannot be immediately purchased with no down payment. Like universities, which respond to the clamor for higher education by tightening their entrance requirements, status groups respond to the clamor by money for prestige by tightening *their* entrance requirements. This phenomenon has been common enough among the wealthiest strata for a long time; money and possessions have rarely been sufficient to admit one to the select circles of old wealth, and the increasingly sharp distinctions between the upper middle class and the lower middle class (which are not merely distinctions of income) suggest that a similar phenomenon may be occurring on lower levels of society.

At one time in recent history, the phrase "middle class" evoked images of Sinclair Lewis, Main Street, *The Saturday Evening Post,* families of smiling faces around brown-turkeyed dinner tables, and a concern with "respectability," but today the phrase is just as likely to evoke images of cocktail parties, country clubs, other-directedness, *The Atlantic Monthly,* Van Gogh prints in wide deep mats, and a hypersensitivity to considerations of status. Sociologists recognize this ambiguity by designating the style suggested by the former series of images as "lower" middle class, and the style suggested by the latter series as "upper" middle class, and tend to think the issue has been clarified. But the conceptual problem implicit in the terminological need to break the middle class into an upper and a lower stratum is too complex to be solved by a simple linguistic device. The problem is not only one of drawing a contemporary line between two contemporary "middle class" styles of life; the immense difference between the life style of the lower middle class and that of the upper middle class also involves a historical dimension.

Nineteenth-century America was a middle-class society in the sense that its typical individuals (if not its statistically modal ones) were shoestring entrepreneurs, and the covers of *The Saturday Evening Post* are a testimony to their former hegemony and to the continuing power of the myth they created. Today, we designate the style of those who follow the lead of the "old" middle class, as "lower" middle class in order to make room for the style of the burgeoning "new" middle class, which we designate as "upper" because this latter style is a tailored, truncated version of an older upper class model emphasizing "taste" and "grace," and made possible—even necessary—by the bright vistas looming before the increasing numbers of college educated people with a promising place in our burgeoning bureaucratic hierarchies. We have no clear images of *American* "working-class style" precisely because the lowest positions on our socioeconomic ladder were traditionally occupied by the most recent groups of European immigrants, each of which, as they arrived, pushed earlier groups of immigrants up. Our images of working-class life, consequently, are dominated by ethnic motifs. But the end of mass immigration from Europe may promote the development of an indigenous white working-class culture in the United States in the near future. Although he feels that it may be premature to dismiss this possibility, S. M. Lipset explains its failure to develop after World War I (when mass immigration from Europe ceased) by reference to the proliferation of new white-collar occupations and to the replacement of European immigration by migrations of labor within the western hemisphere—primarily Mexicans, Puerto Ricans, and Negroes. Nevertheless, the blue-collar work force is likely to remain at between 20 and 25 million for some time to come, and it is extremely doubtful that Mexicans, Puerto Ricans, and Negroes will constitute the major part of this industrial labor force.[3] Moreover, the facts of color, marginal occupations (largely not unionized), and ghetto residence are likely to sustain the ethnicity of these groups for the foreseeable future and isolate them from the native, white working-class culture apparently incipient in the San Jose suburb. For in its visible manifestations, this style seems to approximate the style of the "old" middle class —with a liberal admixture of poor-white southern rural culture. With the gradual disappearance of shopkeepers as a significant stratum in American economic life, the organized well-paid industrial workers (at least our sample of auto workers) seem to have

---

[3] It is true, of course, that, according to recent statistics, the number of people employed in white-collar occupations has for the first time overtaken the number of people employed in blue-collar occupations. See "Labor: A New Social Revolution," *Fortune* (April, 1958), p. 218,

taken over the style of the old middle class with its emphasis on respectability, *without,* however inheriting the mantle of mobility. Even the well-documented yearnings of factory workers for "a little business of my own"—whether or not these yearnings be realistic, nostalgic, or only ritualistic—do not, I think, represent social mobility to them. The major channels of upward mobility today are corporate, and they know this. A gas station, an auto repair shop, a little cafe would surely give them considerably higher prestige among their peers, but it would probably not substantially change their style of life. At worst, it would only make them work longer hours; at best, it would give them only slightly more money. It probably represents only an old-fashioned yearning to be "independent" (the old economic base of the style in which they actually live) and, perhaps, the ever-present impulse to escape the factory.[4] In short, the *lowest* native stratum of substantial size in the American industrial order today (excluding Negroes and marginal workers) probably lives in the style we call "lower middle class."

By my emphasis on the development of a "middle-class working class," I should not be taken to mean that the "lower" class is disappearing; clearly it is not. What I mean is this: that what Warner calls the "upper lower class" (for example, our Ford workers) has less in common with the "lower lower class" than with the "lower middle class." Similarly, the lower middle class has *more* in common with the upper lower class than it has with the upper middle class. For this reason, it seems to me, what Warner calls the "upper lower class" and the "lower middle class" are, in terms of style of life, essentially a single major stratum— *within* which, of course, finer gradations of status will be perceived and acted upon.

It is only in this sense, I think, that America can be called a "middle-class society" and, to be sure, many of our respondents identified themselves as middle class. But as I suggested earlier, our society sanctions this usage, and the myth of suburbia itself

---

[4] To a considerable extent, the concepts "old" and "new" middle class represent the temporal equivalents of the hierarchical "lower" and "upper" middle class. The Lynds and Hans Speier have commented on the tendency for lower strata to assume the life style of the stratum immediately above them in the next generation.

may reinforce the propensity to identify oneself with "America" because America is increasingly characterized in the mass media as a "middle-class society," and the new suburbs are submitted as strong evidence of this. But to call America a middle-class society obscures more than it illumines because the differences between the upper middle class and the lower middle class are too great, both in terms of their cultural style and their economic position, to conceptualize them as different strata of the *same* major class. Indeed, logically, without a substantial "lower" class, "middle" class becomes meaningless. To place a Ford worker, a postman, and a junior engineer at Lockheed in the same "class" represents, if ever anything did, the disappearance of class differences in America.

Nevertheless, it is continually asserted that America is a middle-class society because large segments of its working class take home a pay envelope fat enough to enable them to approximate (and, by virtue of a mechanized domestic life, sometimes to exceed) the style of the old middle class. "Anybody with a steady job and income is middle class," one of my respondents told me, and certainly this is true if we conceive of lower middle-class people as upper middle-class people with slightly lower incomes. For although it is true that these suburbanites I have studied do have only slightly lower incomes than the assistant professor or the junior engineer, it illumines nothing to call them middle class because their style (whether it be designated as working class or as lower middle class) is a *terminal* one; they live in the present, mostly in the style that they have always lived, and mobility is something that is possible only for their children. With a house in the suburbs, two cars, a TV set, a wife and two children, and many major and minor kitchen appliances, one respondent, explaining why he didn't want to be a foreman, said, "I'm a working man. I don't like to be sitting down or walking up and down all the time." Another, explaining why he quit being a foreman after six months, said, "I got nothing against guys in white shirts, but I just ain't cut out for work like that." These are the statements of working class (or, if one insists, lower middle class) men who, because of prosperity and the labor movement, have been able to achieve a standard of living never before possible on any large scale for manual workers. But the element of social mobility is missing; aspiration and anticipation are things for educated people with a fluid position in an organizational hierarchy, and it is this which makes suburban domesticity in a $12,000 house a final fulfillment.

THE FUNCTIONS OF THE MYTH OF SUBURBIA

Why, then, does the myth of suburbia flourish? The appearance of the mass-produced suburbs has been seized upon by the media, mass and otherwise, as a *major phenomenon*, as some sort of fundamental change, not only in ecological structure but in social structure and culture as well—apparently rivaling urbanization and industrialization in the scope of its significance. Suburbia is something to *talk* about—everywhere from the pages of learned journals to best sellers, from academic halls to smoke-filled political rooms to suburban patios and picture-windowed living rooms, and finally now (as if further proof were needed of its significance) to Hollywood. In the movie version of the novel *No Down Payment,* ostensibly a fictional account of life in the new suburbia, Hollywood makes a pointed comment on stratification: the sequence of violence, rape, and accidental death is set in motion by the only important character in the film who is not a white-collar man. Frustrated at being denied the job of police chief (because of his lack of education), the rural, Tennessee-bred service station manager drinks himself into a stupor, rapes his upper-middle class, college-educated neighbor, and then is accidentally killed, symbolically enough, under the wheels of his new Ford. The film closes with his blonde, nymphomaniacal widow leaving the suburb for good on a Sunday morning, while the white collar group is seen leaving the Protestant church (denomination ambiguous) with looks of quiet illumination on their faces.

The flourishing of myths and stereotypes (and, by extension, the image of the age in which they flourish) depends in part upon the availability of visible symbols. The extent, for example, to which the *impact* of juvenile delinquency upon the public consciousness depends not on criminal acts, but on long sideburns, rock and roll, motorcycles, and black leather jackets is worth some research.[5]

---

[5] With striking insight, Harold Rosenberg has observed that "What is remarkable about the manufacture of myths in the twentieth century is that it takes

Similarly, a good part of the peculiar susceptibility of suburbia to the manufacture of myth probably lies in the fact that a large supply of visible symbols are ready at hand. Picture windows, patios and barbecues, power lawn mowers, the problems of commuting, and the armies of children manning their mechanized vehicles down the sidewalks, are only secondarily facts; primarily they are symbols whose function is to evoke an image of a way of life for the nonsuburban public. Presumably, suburbanites know what "suburbia" is like—at least to the extent that the apprehension of such an abstraction is possible. Nevertheless, the myth of suburbia probably also functions to give suburbanites a sense of the "form" of their own lives by dramatically rendering in a public forum the experience of suburbanites, and thus making it historical.[6]

In addition, the visible symbols of suburbia are easily integrated with other aspects of the "spirit" of this "age." Suburbia is the locus of gadgetry, shopping centers, and "station wagon culture"; its grass grows greener, its chrome shines brighter, its lines are clean and new and modern. Suburbia is America in its drip-dry Sunday clothes, standing before the bar of history fulfilled, waiting for its judgment. But like Mr. Dooley's court, which kept its eyes on the election returns, the "judgments" of history are also affected by contemporary ideological currents, and the myth of suburbia flourishes precisely because it is useful as a symbol to widely divergent shades of opinion whose function it is to shape the judgment of history.

Because it is a significant phenomenon, "suburbia" is something upon which men are called to take a stand, much as the "Southern Agrarians" "took their stand" against urbanism and industrialism nearly thirty years ago. To some people suburbia represents the fulfillment of the American middle-class dream; it is identified

---

place under the noses of living witnesses of the actual events and, in fact, cannot dispense with their collaboration." Harold Rosenberg, *The Tradition of the New*, p. 221.

[6] Certainly, suburban self-consciousness is a recent development (together with the myth); as late as 1946, Carl von Rhode was able to say, ". . . the growth of the suburb . . . is one of the remarkable phenomena of our time—and one of which, unfortunately, the suburbanite himself is generally unaware." "The Suburban Mind," *Harper's* (April, 1946), p. 289. Certainly this is no longer true.

with the continuing possibility of upward mobility, with expanding opportunities in middle-class occupations, with rising standards of living and real incomes, and the gadgeted good life as it is reresented in the full-color ads in the mass-circulation magazines. To less sanguine senses, for example, those of some architects, city planners, estheticians, and designers, suburbia represents a dreary blight on the American landscape, the epitome of American standardization and vulgarization, with its row upon monotonous row of mass-produced cheerfulness masquerading as homes, whole agglomerations or "scatterations" of them masquerading as communities. To these eyes, the new tract suburbs of today are the urban slums of tomorrow. There is a third group to whom the myth of suburbia is also important; I mean sociologists and other students of contemporary social and cultural trends. David Riesman says of the authors of *Crestwood Heights* that they "collide, like Whyte, with a problem their predecessors only brushed against, for they are writing about *us*, about the professional upper middle class and its businessman allies, not about a New England museum for the upper class, such as Yankee City, or a small and rather parochial town in the South or Midwest, such as Jonesville or Elmtown. They are writing, as they are almost too aware, about themselves, their friends, their 'type.'" [7] Added to the fascination of professionally studying people who are much like oneself (a kind of positively sanctioned voyeurism), is the tendency to see in suburbia the convergence of some of the apparently major social and cultural trends of our time (other-direction, social mobility, neoconservatism, status anxiety, and the like), thus making of suburbia a microcosm in which the processes at work in the larger society can conveniently be studied. Finally, the vocabularies of some recent left-wing critics of American society seem to have substituted the terms "suburb" and "suburban" for the now embarrassingly obsolete term "bourgeois" as a packaged rebuke to the whole tenor of American life. What used to be condemned as "bourgeois values," "bourgeois style," and "bourgeois hypocrisy" are now simply designated as "suburban."

Although the myth of suburbia is useful to all these groups, it

---

[7] See David Riesman's Introduction to John R. Seeley, *et al.*, *Crestwood Heights: A Study of the Culture of Suburban Life*, p. vii.

cannot be written off simply as ruling class propaganda or as an attempt to see only the sunny side of things, or, for that matter, as an attempt to see only the darker side of things—or even as a furtive attempt to peer into a mirror. Too many responsible intellectuals, though accepting the facts of suburbia, are nevertheless extremely critical of what they see.

But precisely *what* is it that they see that they are critical of? Is it conformity? status anxiety? popular culture? chrome? tail fins? gadgetry? gray flannel suits? No doubt, these are symbols powerful enough to evoke images of an enemy. But the nature of this "enemy" remains peculiarly elusive. Surely, there is nothing specifically suburban about conformity, status anxiety, and the rest, and surely there is nothing diabolical about mass-produced domestic comfort and conservatively cut clothes. It is extraordinary that, with the single exception of William Whyte's attempt to trace "the web of friendship" on the basis of the physical structure of the Park Forest "courts," [8] no one, to my knowledge, has come to grips with the problem of defining what is specifically *suburban* about suburbia. Instead, most writers are reduced to the use of hackneyed stereotypes, not even of suburbia, but of the upper middle class.[9] If, indeed, the images intended to represent suburbia are only symptoms of the commitments of the upper middle class to a way of life whose roots lie conventionally deeper (for example, in the structure of corporate opportunity), then the attack on suburbia may be only a scapegoat phenomenon; suburbia becomes a convenient, safe scapegoat on which to blame the consequences of commitment to chrome idols. Viewed this way, the attack on suburbia has interesting and advantageous consequences for the not-quite-completely-critical intellectual. To heap abuse upon suburbia (instead of upon the ethos of success and the demanding conditions of social and economic mobility) places him comfortably in the great tradition of American social criticism, and at the same time renders him respectable and harmless—because, after all, the critique of suburbia is essentially a

---

[8] See William H. Whyte, Jr., *The Organization Man,* chapter 25.

[9] For example, ". . . out on the suburban frontiers, they are creating a new social order of their own. It is a modern, up-to-date social order, tailored with white-button-down oxford shirts, bow ties, and flannel suits." Louis Harris, *Is There a Republican Majority?* p. 137.

"cultural" critique, not a political or economic one rife with agitational implications. The critic identifies himself by his criticism with culture and taste but at the same time he does not expose himself to the retaliations of powerful political and economic interests, precisely because his criticism constitutes no direct threat to them.[10] Indeed, it may be, as Edward Shils has suggested, that a "cultural" critique is all that is possible today from a left-wing point of view, and certainly the critique of suburbia has about it the same flavor as the critique of mass culture.[11]

But in spite of the string of symbolic epithets that identifies suburbia as the citadel of standardization and vulgarization and conformity, suburbia is testimony to the fact that Americans are living better than ever before. One of the points of this book is to emphasize that this is true not only for white-collar people, but for blue-collar, frayed collar, and turned collar people, also. Today, a family which does not live in a slum is paying upward of 85 or 90 dollars a month in rent, and for this or only slightly more, one can "buy" a new tract home in the suburbs. There is an irony, therefore, in the venom that left-wing critics inject into their discussions of suburbia (as well as of popular culture), not only because Marx himself was aware that a certain level of material satisfaction and leisure were prerequisite to the "leap into freedom," but because, like the criticism of popular culture which Shils has noted, the criticism of suburbia tends to become a criticism of industrialization, "rationality," and "progress," and thus brings these critics quite close to the classic conservatives, whose critique of industrialization was also made in terms of its "cul-

---

[10] The "proletarian literature" of the 1930's had, at the very least, a specific and concrete villain. After reading a proletarian novel or poem of this period, one could at least come away hating the bloated and exploiting "capitalist." Much of the art of the "beat generation" is proletarian too, but the villain has become blurred and diffuse. One comes away hating "them," but who "they" are remains indistinct. For this reason, the mass media can afford to be tolerant and mildly satirical of the "beat generation," whereas the frankly revolutionary literature of the earlier period had to be dealt with more harshly. The Luce magazines, for example, have been prominent also in the satirical treatment of the culture of suburbia—though at the same time emphasizing the great advancements in the standard of living it represents.

[11] See Edward A. Shils, "Daydreams and Nightmares: Reflections on the Criticism of Mass Culture," pp. 587-608.

tural" consequences.[12] It is almost as if left-wing social critics feared the seduction of the working class by pie not in the sky, not even on the table, but in the freezer.

By accepting the myth of suburbia, the liberal and left-wing critics are placed in the ideologically weak position of haranguing the suburbanites precisely for the meaninglessness they attribute to the very criteria of their success. The critic waves the prophet's long and accusing finger and warns: "You may *think* you're happy, you smug and prosperous striver, but I tell you that the anxieties of status mobility are too much; they impoverish you psychologically, they alienate you from your family"; and so on. And the suburbanite looks at his new house, his new car, his new freezer, his lawn and patio, and, to be sure, his good credit, and scratches his head, bewildered. The critic appears as the eternal crotchet, the professional malcontent telling the prosperous that their prosperity, the visible symbols of which surround them, is an illusion: the economic victory of capitalism is culturally Pyrrhic.[13] "Middle-class" symbols have for so long been identified with the enemies of the labor movement, socialism, and the working class, that relatively high standards of living may tend to be perceived as evidence of the disappearance of a real working class instead of as *conditions* capable of generating a consciousness of collective achievement which is worth fighting to preserve.

---

[12] Exceptions are Disraeli, the early Churchill, and a few other English conservatives, who tried to unite the gentry and the working classes against the middle classes. See, for example, Peter Viereck's discussion of this in *Conservatism, from John Adams to Churchill*, pp. 42-45.

[13] A typical example of this view is Erich Fromm's discussion of Park Forest in *The Sane Society*, pp. 152-162.

Appendix I
TABLES

NOTE ON THE TABLES

Since the sample on which this study is based is comparatively small, the statistical tables must be interpreted with caution. The probability is small that exactly the same set of sample measures would result from other sample surveys, even if the samples studied were selected in such a way as to include somewhat similar groups of working-class suburbanites. Especially when the base of a percentage is unusually small—say, eight or a dozen cases—the percentage must be regarded as particularly subject to sampling error.

TABLE A.1

Estimates of Chances of Getting Ahead
(Percentages)

Categories	Good	Fair	Not much chance	Total per cent	Number of respondents
BY AGE GROUPS					
20-29................	23	64	14	101	22
30-39................	23	44	33	100	39
40-49................	6	29	65	100	31
50 plus.............	12	0	88	100	8
BY PLACE OF BIRTH					
Urban...............	24	53	24	101	29
Rural...............	15	32	52	99	65
Foreign.............	0	67	33	100	6
BY JOB STATUS					
Skilled..............	0	33	67	100	9
Semiskilled (line)....	8	38	54	100	50
Semiskilled (non-line)	15	46	38	99	26
Foremen.............	58	42	0	100	12
BY LAST GRADE COMPLETED IN SCHOOL					
1-8.................	5	28	67	100	39
9-11................	17	49	34	100	35
12 or more..........	35	46	19	100	26
TOTAL SAMPLE					
	17	40	43	100	100

TABLE A.2

Expectations of Promotion to Foreman[a]
(*Percentages*)

Categories	Yes	No	Don't know	Total per cent	Number of respondents
BY AGE GROUPS					
20-29...............	28	39	33	100	18
30-39...............	28	56	16	100	32
40-49...............	7	70	23	100	30
50 plus.............	0	100	0	100	7
BY LAST GRADE COMPLETED IN SCHOOL					
1-8.................	8	79	13	100	38
9-11................	27	50	23	100	30
12 or more..........	26	42	32	100	19
BY PLACE OF BIRTH					
Urban...............	30	39	30	99	23
Rural...............	16	67	17	100	58
Foreign.............	0	83	17	100	6
TOTAL SAMPLE					
	21	54	26	101	87

[a] Excludes those who are already foremen.

TABLE A.3

PERMANENCE OF HOME

(*Percentages*)

Categories	Permanent	Expect to move	Don't know	Total per cent	Number of respondents
	BY AGE GROUPS				
20-29..............	55	45	0	100	22
30-39..............	77	15	8	100	39
40-49..............	81	13	6	100	31
	BY JOB STATUS				
Skilled.............	67	22	11	100	9
Semiskilled (line)....	84	14	2	100	50
Semiskilled (non-line)	77	19	4	100	26
Foremen............	33	50	17	100	12
	TOTAL SAMPLE				
	73	21	6	100	100

TABLE A.4

OCCUPATIONAL PREFERENCES OF PARENTS
FOR CHILDREN

OCCUPATIONS AND NUMBER OF TIMES MENTIONED

Engineer..	8
Doctor...	4
Professional ball player............................	3
"Scientist"..	3
"Trade or a good position".........................	2
"A profession"....................................	2
Psychologist.......................................	1
TV technician.....................................	1
"It's up to him"..................................	30
Don't know.......................................	11

TABLE A.5

Voting Record
(*Percentages*)

	Year		
Record	1956 (*100 respondents*)	1952 (*100 respondents*)	1948 (*100 respondents*)
Democratic............	64	53	50
Republican............	14	19	5
Did not vote...........	19	20	16
Not eligible............	3	8	27
Don't remember........	...	...	2
Totals.............	100	100	100

TABLE A.6

Political Identification
(*Percentages*)

Categories	Democratic	Republican	Independent	Don't know	Total per cent	Number in sample
BY TYPE OF FORMER RESIDENCE						
Homeowners.....	81	13	6	...	100	31
Renters (pvt.)....	79	14	3	3	99	29
Renters (gov.)[a]...	82	8	8	2	100	40
BY AGE GROUPS						
20-29...........	68	19	9	5	100	22
30-39...........	85	3	10	3	101	39
40-49...........	90	10	...	...	100	31
50 plus.........	62	38	...	...	100	8
TOTAL SAMPLE						
	81	11	6	2	100	100

[a] The 40 respondents listed as "Renters (gov.)" include two who lived in run-down Richmond hotels before the movement of the plant.

TABLE A.7

VOTING RECORD BY LAST GRADE COMPLETED IN SCHOOL
(*Percentages*)

Categories	1-8 (*39 respondents*)	9-11 (*35 respondents*)	12 or more (*26 respondents*)
1956			
Stevenson........	74	63	50
Eisenhower.......	10	9	27
Did not vote......	13	26	19
Not eligible.......	3	3	4
Totals..........	100	101	100
1952			
Stevenson.........	67	57	27
Eisenhower.......	8	17	38
Did not vote......	21	14	27
Not eligible.......	5	11	8
Totals..........	101	99	100
1948			
Truman..........	67	46	31
Dewey...........	3	6	8
Did not vote......	21	14	12
Don't remember...	3	3	0
Not eligible.......	8	31	50
Totals..........	102	100	101

TABLE A.8

INTEREST IN POLITICS
(*Percentages*)

	Type of former residence		
Degree of interest	Homeowners (*31 respondents*)	Renters (pvt.) (*29 respondents*)	Renters (gov.) (*40 respondents*)
Very interested..........	19	3	5
Moderately interested....	39	31	42
Hardly interested at all...	42	66	52
Totals...............	100	100	99

TABLE A.9

RELATIVE INTEREST IN POLITICS SINCE MOVE TO SUBURBS
(*Percentages*)

Categories	More interested	Less interested	About the same	Total per cent	Number of respondents
BY POLITICAL IDENTIFICATION					
Democratic........	32	4	64	100	81
Republican.........	0	27	73	100	11
Independent.......	38	0	62	100	8
BY TYPE OF FORMER RESIDENCE					
Homeowners.......	13	6	81	100	31
Renters (pvt.)......	34	7	59	100	29
Renters (gov.)......	38	5	58	101	40
TOTAL SAMPLE					
	29	6	65	100	100

TABLE A.10

CHURCH ATTENDANCE

(Percentages)

Categories	Never	Rarely	Some-times	Often	Every Sunday	Total per cent	Number in sample
			BY DENOMINATION				
Catholic.........	9	43	9	9	30	100	23
"Protestant"ᵃ....	61	17	13	4	4	99	23
Baptist.........	23	9	9	27	32	100	22
Other Protestant	36	12	28	4	20	100	25
			BY AGE GROUPS				
20-29...........	45	18	18	...	18	99	22
30-39...........	38	15	10	8	28	99	39
40-49...........	29	23	16	19	13	100	31
50 plus.........	25	38	12	12	12	99	8
		BY LAST GRADE COMPLETED IN SCHOOL					
1-8.............	31	23	13	10	23	100	39
9-11...........	34	23	14	14	14	99	35
12 or more......	46	12	15	4	23	100	26
		BY TYPE OF FORMER RESIDENCE					
Homeowners.....	35	23	13	6	23	100	31
Renters (pvt.)...	45	14	21	10	10	100	29
Renters (gov.)...	30	22	10	12	25	99	40
			TOTAL SAMPLE				
	36	20	14	10	20	100	100

ᵃ No denomination given.

TABLE A.11

Comparative Frequency of Church Attendance
(*Percentages*)

In suburb	More often	Less often	About the same	Total per cent	Number of respondents
	BY TYPE OF FORMER RESIDENCE				
Homeowners.......	19	29	52	100	31
Renters (pvt.)......	21	34	45	100	29
Renters (gov.)......	38	12	50	100	40
	BY DENOMINATION				
Catholic...........	22	30	48	100	23
"Protestant"[a]......	22	22	57	101	23
Baptist............	45	23	32	100	22
Other Protestant....	28	28	44	100	25
	TOTAL SAMPLE				
	27	24	49	100	100

[a] No denomination given.

TABLE A.12

Perception of Relative Frequency
of Church Attendance of Community
(*Percentages*)

Categories	More often	Less often	About the same	Don't know	Total per cent	Number in sample
	BY TYPE OF FORMER RESIDENCE					
Homeowners....	29	32	19	19	99	31
Renters (pvt.)..	34	31	31	3	99	29
Renters (gov.)..	58	7	33	2	100	40
	BY COMPARATIVE FREQUENCY OF CHURCH ATTENDANCE					
More often.....	56	7	33	4	100	27
Less often......	17	50	25	8	100	24
About the same.	47	16	27	10	100	49
	TOTAL SAMPLE					
	42	22	28	8	100	100

TABLE A.13

MEMBERSHIPS IN ORGANIZATIONS
(Percentages)

Categories	Organizations				Total per cent	Number of respondents
	0	1	2	3		
BY PLACE OF BIRTH						
Urban...............	79	21	0	0	100	29
Rural...............	66	23	5	6	100	65
Foreign..............	67	17	17	0	101	6
BY AGE GROUPS						
21-29...............	68	27	0	5	100	22
30-39...............	64	21	8	8	101	39
40-49...............	77	19	3	0	99	31
50plus	75	25	0	0	100	8
BY TYPE OF FORMER RESIDENCE						
Homeowner..........	74	19	3	3	99	31
Renters (pvt.)........	66	31	0	3	100	29
Renters (gov.).......	70	18	8	5	101	40
BY LAST GRADE COMPLETED IN SCHOOL						
1-8................	74	15	8	3	100	39
9-11...............	63	31	3	3	100	35
12 or more..........	73	19	0	8	100	26
BY JOB STATUS						
Skilled..............	78	22	0	0	100	9
Semiskilled (line)......	68	26	2	4	100	50
Semiskilled (non-line)..	69	23	8	0	100	26
Foremen.............	83	8	0	8	99	12
TOTAL SAMPLE						
	70	22	4	4	100	100

TABLE A.14

FREQUENCY OF ENTERTAINING BY TYPE OF RESIDENCE
(*Percentages*)

Frequency of "having people in"	Type of former residence		
	Homeowner (*31 respondents*)	Renter (pvt.) (*29 respondents*)	Renter (gov.) (*40 respondents*)
About once a week.........	45	34	35
About once a month.......	32	48	40
About once in 6 months....	16	17	20
About once a year.........	3	0	5
Never..................	3	0	0
Totals.................	99	99	100

TABLE A.15

COMPARATIVE FREQUENCY OF ENTERTAINING IN SUBURB
(*Percentages*)

Categories	More often	Less often	About the same	Total per cent	Number of respondents
BY TYPE OF FORMER RESIDENCE					
Homeowner........	26	39	35	100	31
Renter (pvt.).......	45	21	34	100	29
Renter (gov.).......	42	22	35	99	40
BY LAST GRADE COMPLETED IN SCHOOL					
1-8...............	39	21	39	99	39
9-11..............	42	31	28	101	35
12 or more.........	31	31	38	100	26
TOTAL SAMPLE					
	38	7	35	100	100

TABLE A.16

OCCUPATIONS OF FRIENDS AND NEIGHBORS OF RESPONDENTS

(*Percentages*)

Occupation	Two closest friends	Two closest neighbors
Ford workers...................	43.0	31.5
Ford foremen...................	4.5	2.0
Semiskilled labor...............	10.0	18.5
Skilled labor, foremen..........	13.0	17.5
Salesmen......................	2.5	3.5
Businessmen...................	3.5	2.0
Prof. or semiprof..............	9.5	5.5
Lower white collar.............	8.5	9.5
Servicemen (military) or students	0.5	3.0
Widows or divorcees............	0.0	2.0
Retired.......................	0.5	0.5
Don't know...................	4.5	4.5
Totals.....................	100.0	100.0

TABLE A.17

FREQUENCY OF GOING OUT BY DEGREE OF EDUCATION

(*Percentages*)

How often do you "go out" on weekends?	Last grade completed in school		
	1-8 (*39 respondents*)	9-11 (*35 respondents*)	12 or more (*26 respondents*)
Never....................	5	0	8
Rarely...................	71	44	31
Sometimes...............	16	33	31
Often...................	8	22	31
Totals.................	100	99	101

TABLE A.18

FREQUENCY OF PARTYGOING FOR HUSBAND AND WIFE
(*Percentages*)

Categories	Never	Rarely	Some-times	Total per cent	Number of respondents
BY LAST GRADE COMPLETED IN SCHOOL					
1-8................	59	36	5	100	39
9-11...............	46	40	14	100	35
12 or more.........	27	38	35	100	26
BY AGE GROUPS					
20-29..............	36	45	18	100	22
30-39..............	41	41	18	100	39
40-49..............	55	32	13	100	31
50 plus............	63	25	12	100	8
TOTAL SAMPLE					
	46	38	16	100	100

TABLE A.19

MOVIE ATTENDANCE

Category	Never	Rarely	Some-times	Often	Total per cent	Number of respondents
BY LAST GRADE COMPLETED IN SCHOOL						
1-8............	16	53	24	8	101	39
9-11...........	8	42	31	19	100	35
12 or more......	0	38	42	19	99	26
TOTAL SAMPLE						
	9	45	31	15	100	100

TABLE A.20

Hours Per Week at TV
(*100 respondents*)

Hours	Per cent
0-5	8
6-10	26
11-15	19
16-20	21
21 plus	26
Total	100

TABLE A.21

Self-Rankings
(*Percentages*)

Class	Self-rankings	
	In Richmond (*100 respondents*)	In the suburb (*100 respondents*)
Upper middle[a]	1	3
Middle	31	36
Working	53	48
Lower	3	1
"Average" or "Medium"	9	9
Lower middle	2	2
Don't know	1	1
Totals	100	100

[a] The questions on which the class designations are based represent neither forced choice nor completely open-ended questions. The questions were formulated in an open-ended way. Frequently, however, the respondent asked for examples of the kind of answer desired, and the interviewer responded by saying "Well, you know, Middle Class, Working Class, Lower Class, something like that."

TABLE A.22

RANKINGS OF NEIGHBORS
(*Percentages*)

Class	Rankings of neighbors	
	In Richmond (*100 respondents*)	In the suburb (*100 respondents*)
Upper middle...............	1	0
Middle......................	24	35
Working....................	49	50
Lower......................	12	2
"Average" or "medium"........	9	9
Lower middle...............	2	2
Don't know.................	3	2
Totals.....................	100	100

TABLE A.23

RANKING OF NEIGHBORS BY TYPE OF RESIDENCE
(*Percentages*)

Class of neighbors before the move	Type of former residence		
	Homeowners (*31 respondents*)	Renters (pvt.) (*29 respondents*)	Renters (gov.) (*40 respondents*)
Upper middle............	3	0	0
Middle..................	32	28	15
Working.................	52	52	45
Lower...................	3	7	23
"Average" or "medium"....	3	10	12
Lower middle............	3	0	2
Don't know..............	3	3	2
Totals..................	99	100	99

TABLE A.24

COMPARATIVE RANKINGS OF NEIGHBORS
(*Percentages*)

Comparative rankings of present with former neighbors	Type of former residence		
	Homeowners (*31 respondents*)	Renters (pvt.) (*29 respondents*)	Renters (gov.) (*40 respondents*)
Higher class...............	10	17	42
Lower class...............	13	0	0
About the same...........	74	79	55
Don't know	3	3	3
Totals................	100	99	100

TABLE A.25

SELF-RANKING IN RICHMOND
(*Percentages*)

Categories	Upper middle	Middle	Working	Lower	Average or medium	Lower middle	Don't know	Total per cent	No. in sample
BY TYPE OF FORMER RESIDENCE									
Homeowners...	3	35	55	0	3	3	0	99	31
Renters (pvt.) .	0	28	55	3	10	3	0	99	29
Renters (gov.) .	0	30	50	5	12	0	2	99	40
BY LAST GRADE COMPLETED IN SCHOOL									
1-8..........	3	23	62	8	5	0	0	101	39
9-11..........	0	31	54	0	11	0	3	99	35
12 or more....	0	42	38	0	12	8	0	100	26
BY PLACE OF BIRTH									
Rural.........	0	29	57	5	8	0	2	101	65
Urban........	3	38	45	0	10	3	0	99	29
Foreign.......	0	17	50	0	17	17	0	101	6
TOTAL SAMPLE									
	1	21	53	3	9	2	1	100	100

TABLE A.26

Self-Ranking in the Suburb
(*Percentages*)

Categories	Upper middle	Middle	Working	Lower	Average or medium	Lower middle	Don't know	Total per cent	No. in sample
BY LAST GRADE COMPLETED IN SCHOOL									
1-8..........	3	31	59	3	5	0	0	101	39
9-11..........	3	37	46	0	11	0	3	100	35
12 or more....	4	42	35	0	12	8	0	101	26
BY PLACE OF BIRTH									
Rural.........	3	34	42	2	7	0	2	100	65
Urban........	3	45	38	0	10	3	0	99	29
Foreign.......	0	17	50	0	17	17	0	101	6
BY JOB STATUS									
Skilled........	0	44	44	0	11	0	0	99	9
Semiskilled.... (line)	2	36	52	2	4	2	2	100	50
Semiskilled.... (non-line)	0	35	46	0	15	4	0	100	26
Foremen......	17	33	50	0	0	0	0	100	12
TOTAL SAMPLE									
	3	36	48	1	9	2	1	100	100

TABLE A.27

How Much Power Does Labor Have?

(Percentages)

Categories	Too much	Too little	About right	Don't know	Total per cent	Number in sample
BY LAST GRADE COMPLETED IN SCHOOL						
1-8............	8	44	46	3	101	39
9-11............	20	26	54	0	100	35
12 or more......	19	19	58	4	100	26
BY AGE GROUPS						
20-29..........	18	23	59	0	100	22
30-39..........	23	23	49	5	100	39
40-49..........	0	42	58	0	100	31
50 plus.........	25	50	25	0	100	8
BY JOB STATUS						
Skilled.........	11	22	67	0	100	9
Semiskilled..... (line)	10	32	56	2	100	50
Semiskilled..... (non-line)	12	42	42	4	100	26
TOTAL SAMPLE						
	15	31	52	2	100	100

Appendix II

THE INTERVIEW SCHEDULE

INSTITUTE OF INDUSTRIAL RELATIONS

University of California
Berkeley 4, California

SAN JOSE FORD SURVEY

Date _____   # _____

I. *Satisfaction with the Move*

1. How long have you been living here? _____
2. If you had been able to vote on whether or not the plant should move, before it actually did, how would you have voted?
   (1) For _____ (2) Against _____ (3) DK _____
3. Why would you have voted this way? _____
4. How do you feel about the move now; was it a good thing for you?
   (1) Pro _____ (2) Con _____ (3) Indifferent _____
   (4) Mixed feelings _____
5. When you worked in the Richmond plant, did you own your own home, rent a house or apartment, or did you rent one of the government project apartments?
   (1) Own Home _____ (2) Rent House or Apt. _____
   (3) Rent Gov't. Apt. _____
6. Is your present housing an improvement over your former housing?
   (1) Better _____ (2) Worse _____ (3) About the same _____
7. In general, is this a very good, a fairly good, or a not at all good community to live in?
   (1) Very good _____ (2) Fairly good _____ (3) Not at all good _____
8. In what ways is living in this community better than living in the Richmond area? _____
9. In what ways was living in the Richmond area better than living in this community? _____
10. Would you say, from your experience, that the advantages of owning your own home outweigh the disadvantages or vice-versa?
    (1) Advantages outweigh _____ (2) Disadvantages outweigh _____ (3) Don't know _____
11. Why do you feel this way? _____

II. *Mobility*

12. How much movement of families in and out of this neighborhood is there?
    (1) Very much _____   (2) A moderate amount _____
    (3) Hardly any _____

13. Do you think of your job with Ford as a permanent one or are you keeping your eye open for something different?
    (1) Permanent with Ford _____   (2) Looking for something different _____   (3) Other _____ (Explain) _____
    _____

14. How good a chance do you think you have of getting ahead in your present job?
    (1) A good chance _____   (2) A fairly good chance _____
    (3) Not much chance _____

15. Have you ever been a foreman? _____; 15.a. Would you like to be one? _____; 15.b. Do you ever expect to be one? _____

16. Do you ever expect to be a manager or an executive of some kind?
    _____

17. Have you ever owned your own business? _____; 17.a. Have you ever wanted to? _____

18. Do you think of your home here as a relatively permanent one or do you expect to move within the foreseeable future?
    (1) Relatively permanent _____   (2) Expect to move _____
    (3) Don't know _____

19. What would you say is an adequate monthly income for a family of four?
    (1) $200-299 _____   (2) $300-399 _____   (3) $400-499
    _____   (4) $500-599 _____   (5) $600- _____

20. Do you think that most of your neighbors are better off, worse off, or in about the same financial situation as you are?
    (1) Better off _____   (2) Worse off _____   (3) About the same _____   (4) Don't know _____

21. When you worked in the Richmond plant, did you bring your lunch, or buy it in the cafeteria?
    (1) Brought lunch _____   (2) Bought lunch _____   (3) 50-50 _____

22. Do you bring your lunch with you now or do you buy it in the cafeteria?
    (1) Bring lunch _____   (2) Buy lunch _____   (3) 50-50
    _____

III. *Child Rearing*

23. How many children do you have? _____
    Ages of boys _____ _____ _____ _____
    Ages of girls _____ _____ _____ _____
24. How far would you like your son (sons) to go in school?
    (1) Some high school _____ (2) H. S. graduation _____
    (3) Some college _____ (4) College graduation _____
    (5) Don't know _____
25. (If sons are grown) How far did your sons go in school?
    _____ _____ _____ _____

26. (If sons are grown) What occupation(s) does (do) your son(s) have?
    _____

27. (If sons are not grown) What occupation(s) would you like him (them) to follow? _____
28. Have you or your wife ever read any books on child rearing? ___
    28.a. Do you remember any of their names? _____
29. (If yes) Do you or your wife ever engage in any discussion of these books with friends? _____
30. To what extent have you become friendly with the parents of your children's friends? (1) Not at all _____ (2) Somewhat _____ (3) Very much _____

IV. *Informal Social Relations*

31. How many new friends have you and your wife made since you've been living here?
    (1) Hardly any _____ (2) Some _____ (3) Many _____
32. Are they mostly from the plant, the neighborhood, or somewhere else?
    (1) Plant _____ (2) Neighborhood _____ (3) Other _____ (Specify) _____
33. What are the occupations of your two closest friends?
    (1) _____ (2) _____
34. What are the occupations of your two closest neighbors?
    (1) _____ (2) _____
35. How friendly are you with your two closest neighbors?
    (1) Very friendly _____ (2) Moderately friendly _____
    (3) Barely friendly _____

36. When you lived in the Richmond area, how often did you and your wife entertain friends at home?
(1) About once a week _____ (2) About once a month _____ (3) About once in six months _____ (4) About once in a year _____

37. Do you entertain friends at home more or less frequently than you did in the Richmond area?
(1) More frequently _____ (2) Less frequently _____ (3) About the same _____

38. (If wife is present, ask her) How often do you visit other housewives during the day?
(1) Hardly ever _____ (2) Occasionally _____ (3) Often _____

39. How often do other housewives drop in on you during the day?
(1) Hardly ever _____ (2) Occasionally _____ (3) Often _____

40. How many friends do you and your wife have who still live in the Richmond area?
(1) Hardly any _____ (2) Some _____ (3) Many _____ (4) None _____

41. How often do you see them?
(1) Rarely _____ (2) Occasionally _____ (3) Often _____

42. How often do you and your wife visit:
a. Neighbors? (1) Rarely _____ (2) Occasionally _____ (3) Often _____
b. Relatives? (1) Rarely _____ (2) Occasionally _____ (3) Often _____
c. Friends from the plant? (1) Rarely _____ (2) Occasionally _____ (3) Often _____
d. Friends who are neither neighbors nor fellow workers (specify) _____ (1) Rarely _____ (2) Occasionally _____ (3) Often _____

43. How often do you and your wife "go out"?
(1) Rarely _____ (2) Occasionally _____ (3) Often _____

44. When you do go out what do you do most frequently?
_____

45. Do you and your wife go out more or less frequently than you did when you lived in the Richmond area?

(1) More frequently _____   (2) Less frequently _____
(3) About the same _____

46. How often do you go out without your wife, for example to spend an evening "out with the boys"?
(1) Never _____   (2) Occasionally _____   (3) Often

_____

V. *Politics*

47. Did you vote in 1956? _____; 47.a. In 1952? _____; 47.b. In 1948? _____

48. Do you remember how you voted in the presidential election last year? Was it for Eisenhower or Stevenson?
(1) Eisenhower _____   (2) Stevenson _____

49. What about 1952? Did you vote for Eisenhower or Stevenson then?
(1) Eisenhower _____   (2) Stevenson _____
(3) Other _____

50. In general, do you consider yourself to be a Republican, a Democrat, or an Independent?
(1) Republican _____   (2) Democrat _____   (3) Independent _____

51. In 1948, there were four major candidates, Dewey, Truman, Thurmond, and Wallace; do you remember whom you voted for that year?
(1) Dewey _____   (2) Truman _____   (3) Wallace _____   (4) Thurmond _____   (5) Other _____

52. How interested would you say you are in politics?
(1) Very interested _____   (2) Moderately interested _____
(3) Hardly interested at all _____

53. Since leaving the Richmond area, have you become any more or less interested in politics?
(1) More interested _____   (2) Less interested _____
(3) Same _____

54. When you lived in the Richmond area, were most of your neighbors Republicans, Democrats, or Independents?
(1) Republicans _____   (2) Democrats _____   (3) Independents _____   (4) Don't know _____   (5) 50-50

_____

55. What do you think most of the people are in this neighborhood?
(1) Republican _____   (2) Democrat _____   (3) Inde-

pendent _____ (4) Don't know _____ (5) 50-50

_____

56. Do your two closest friends generally consider themselves Republicans, Democrats, or Independents?
    (1) Republicans _____ (2) Democrats _____ (3) Independents _____
57. Did your parents think of themselves as Republicans, Democrats, or Independents?
    (1) Republican _____ (2) Democrat _____ (3) Independent _____ (4) Don't know _____
58. How does your wife usually vote?
    (1) Republican _____ (2) Democrat _____ (3) Independent _____ (4) Other _____
59. Whom did she vote for last year?
    (1) Eisenhower _____ (2) Stevenson _____

VI. *Organizations*

60. Do you belong to any clubs, lodges, or associations?
    _____; 60.a. Which ones? _____
61. Do you belong to more or fewer organizations now than you did when you lived in the Richmond area?
    (1) More _____ (2) Fewer _____ (3) About the same

    _____

62. How frequently do you attend meetings of organizations to which you belong?
    (1) Rarely _____ (2) Occasionally _____ (3) Often

    _____

63. Do you attend meetings now more or less frequently than you did in the Richmond area?
    (1) More frequently _____ (2) Less frequently _____
    (3) Same _____
64. What organizations does your wife belong to?

    _____

65. How frequently does she attend meetings?
    (1) Rarely _____ (2) Occasionally _____ (3) Often

    _____

66. Does she belong to more or fewer organizations now than she did in the Richmond area?
    (1) More _____ (2) Fewer _____ (3) About the same

    _____

67. How often do you attend union meetings?

(1) Rarely _____   (2) Occasionally _____   (3) Often
_____

68. Are there any civic or neighborhood improvement associations
around here? _____;   68.a. Do you belong? _____;   68.b.
(If not) Why? _____

VII. *Recreation and Leisure*

69. Do you own a TV set? _____
70. Did you in Richmond? _____
71. About how many hours a week do you watch TV? _____
72. What are your three favorite programs?   (1) _____
(2) _____   (3) _____
73. How often do you go to the movies?
(1) Rarely _____   (2) Sometimes _____   (3) Often
_____

73.a. More or less than in Richmond?
(1) More _____   (2) Less _____   (3) Same _____
74. When you lived in Richmond, did you and your wife subscribe
to any magazines? _____;   74.a. Which ones _____
75. What magazines do you subscribe to now? _____
76. How often do you and your wife go to parties here in this neighborhood?
(1) Never _____   (2) Rarely _____   (3) Sometimes
_____   (4) Often _____
77. Do you and your wife ever have a cocktail before dinner?
(1) Never _____   (2) Rarely _____   (3) Sometimes
_____   (4) Often _____
78. Did you when you lived in the Richmond area? _____
(1) More often _____   (2) Less often _____   (3) Same
_____

79. Do you ever have beer or wine with dinner? _____
Beer: (1) Never _____   (2) Rarely _____   (3) Sometimes _____   (4) Often _____
Wine: (5) Never _____   (6) Rarely _____   (7) Sometimes _____   (8) Often _____
80. Did you when you lived in the Richmond area? _____
Beer: (1) More often _____   (2) Less Often _____
(3) About the same _____
Wine: (4) More often _____   (5) Less often _____
(6) About the same _____

81. Would you say that you drink more now or less than you did when you lived in the Richmond area?
    (1) More _____ (2) Less _____ (3) About the same
    _____

VIII. *Religion*

82. About how often do you attend church?
    (1) Never _____ (2) Rarely _____ (3) Sometimes
    _____ (4) Often _____ (5) Every week _____
    82.a. Does your wife attend church more or less often than you?
    (1) More often _____ (2) Less often _____ (3) Same
    _____

83. Do you go to church here more or less often than you did in the Richmond area?
    (1) More often _____ (2) Less often _____ (3) About the same _____

84. Have you ever discussed any of your family problems with your clergyman? _____ 84.a. Did you when you lived in the Richmond area? _____

85. Would you say that people go to church more or less often around here than your neighbors did in Richmond?
    (1) More _____ (2) Less _____ (3) Same _____

86. Besides going to religious services, how often do you participate in other church activities?
    (1) Never _____ (2) Rarely _____ (3) Sometimes
    _____ (4) Often _____

87. Which do you feel is more important to the welfare of you and your family, your union membership or your church membership?
    (1) Union _____ (2) Church _____ (3) Don't know
    _____

88. Since leaving Richmond, has membership in a church become any more or less important to you?
    (1) More _____ (2) Less _____ (3) Same _____

IX. *Class Consciousness*

89. When you lived in the Richmond area, what social class did you think of yourself as belonging to?
    (1) UM _____ (2) M _____ (3) W _____ (4) L
    _____ (5) Other _____

90. Do you feel the same way, or do you think of yourself as belonging to another social class down here?

(1) UM _____ (2) M _____ (3) W _____ (4) L _____ (5) Other _____

91. Do you think your neighbors around here are higher or lower class than your neighbors were in the Richmond area?
(1) Higher _____ (2) Lower _____ (3) Same _____ (4) Don't know _____

92. In what class do you think most of your neighbors around here belong?
(1) UM _____ (2) M _____ (3) W _____ (4) L _____ (5) Other _____

93. In what class do you think most of your Richmond neighbors belonged?
(1) UM _____ (2) M _____ (3) W _____ (4) L _____ (5) Other _____

94. Are there any particular organizations or groups whose opinion you usually trust on political questions? _____; 94.a. Which ones? _____

95. Do you think that Labor has too much power, too little power, or just about the right amount of power?
(1) Too much _____ (2) Too little _____ (3) About right _____

X. *Biographical*

96. May I ask your age? _____

97. Where were you born? _____
(1) City of over 100,000 or suburb _____ (2) City of 2500-100,000 _____ (3) Town under 2500 _____ (4) Farm _____

98. Where was your father born? _____

99. Where was your mother born? _____

100. What was the last grade you completed in school?
(1) None _____ (2) 1-6 _____ (3) 7-8 _____ (4) 9-11 _____ (5) 12 _____ (6) College, non-grad _____ (7) College graduate _____

101. Are you (1) Married _____ (2) Single _____ (3) Widowed _____ (4) Divorced _____

102. What was the last grade your wife completed in school?
(1) None _____ (2) 1-6 _____ (3) 7-8 _____ (4) 9-11 _____ (5) 12 _____ (6) College, non-grad _____ (7) College graduate _____

103. What is your religious preference? (1) Catholic _____

(2) Jewish _____ (3) Protestant (denomination) _____
(4) Other _____

104. What is your job with Ford? _____
(1) Skilled _____ (2) Semi-skilled, line _____ (3)
Semi-skilled, non-line _____ (4) Foreman _____ (5)
Other _____

105. How long have you worked for Ford?
(1) 1-5 _____ (2) 6-10 _____ (3) 11-15 _____
(4) 16-20 _____ (5) 21 plus _____

106. What is (was) your father's main occupation in his life? _____

107. Have you ever held a full time white collar job? _____ 107.a.
When and for how long? _____

108. Does your wife work? _____ (if yes) (1) Full time _____
(2) Part time _____ (3) Occasionally or seasonally _____

109. Did your wife work when you lived in the Richmond area? _____
(if yes) (1) full time _____ (2) Part time _____
(3) Occasionally or seasonally _____

110. For the purposes of our survey, we need to have a rough indication of your family's weekly take-home pay. Would you mind
telling me which of the following figures it comes closest to?
(1) $50 _____ (2) $60 _____ (3) $70 _____ (4)
$80 _____ (5) $90 _____ (6) $100 _____ (7)
$125 _____ (8) $150 _____

REMARKS _____
_____
_____

Bibliography

Bibliography

Allen, Frederick Lewis. "The Big Change in Suburbia, Part I." *Harper's*, June, 1954, pp. 21-28.
———. "The Big Change in Suburbia, Part II, Crisis in the Suburbs." *Harper's*, July, 1954, pp. 47-53.
Beegle, J. Allen. "Characteristics of Michigan's Fringe Population." *Rural Sociology*, September, 1947, pp. 254-263.
Bell, Wendell, and Maryanne T. Force. "Social Structure and Participation in Different Types of Formal Associations." *Social Forces*, May, 1956, pp. 345-350.
———. "Urban Neighborhood Types and Participation in Formal Associations." *American Sociological Review*, February, 1956, pp. 25-34.
Bogue, Donald. *Population Growth in Standard Metropolitan Areas, 1900-1950*. Washington, D. C.: U. S. Government Printing Office, 1953.
Bridenbaugh, Carl. *Cities in Revolt: Urban Life in America, 1743-1776*. New York: Alfred A. Knopf, 1955.
Bridgman, H. A. "The Suburbanite." *Independent*, April 10, 1902, pp. 862-864.
Brunner, Edmund deS., and Wilbur C. Hallenbeck. *American Society: Urban and Rural Patterns*. New York: Harper & Brothers, 1955.
Burton, Hal. "Trouble in the Suburbs." *The Saturday Evening Post*, September 17, 1955, pp. 19-21, 113-118.
Campbell, Angus, *et al., The Voter Decides*. Evanston: Row, Peterson Company, n.d. (1954)
Chinoy, Eli. *Automobile Workers and the American Dream*. New York: Doubleday & Co., 1955.

Cuzzort, Raymond. *Suburbanization of Service Industries Within Standard Metropolitan Areas.* Miami, Ohio: The Scripps Foundation, 1955.

Dobriner, William (ed.). *The Suburban Community.* New York: G. P. Putnam's Sons, 1958.

Dotson, Floyd. "Patterns of Voluntary Association Among Urban Working Class Families." *American Sociological Review,* October, 1951, pp. 687-693.

Douglass, Harlan P. *The Suburban Trend.* New York: D. Appleton Century Co., 1925.

Durkheim, Emile. *Suicide.* Glencoe, Illinois: The Free Press, 1951.

———. *The Elementary Forms of the Religious Life.* Glencoe, Illinois: The Free Press, 1947.

Fava, Sylvia. "Suburbanism as a Way of Life." *American Sociological Review,* February, 1956, pp. 34-37.

"Flight to the Suburbs." *Time,* March 22, 1954, p. 102.

Frederick, Christine. "Is Suburban Living a Delusion?" *Outlook,* February 22, 1928, pp. 290-291, 313.

Fromm, Erich. *The Sane Society.* London: Routledge and Kegan Paul, 1956.

Galbraith, John K. *The Affluent Society.* Boston: Houghton Mifflin Co., 1958.

Gersh, Harry. "The New Suburbanites of the 50's." *Commentary,* March, 1954, pp. 209-221.

Gist, Noel P. "Developing Patterns of Urban Decentralization." *Social Forces,* March, 1952, pp. 257-267.

Goldschmidt, Walter. "Social Class and the Dynamics of Status in America." *American Anthropologist,* December, 1955, pp. 1209-1217.

Greeley, Andrew M. "Suburbia, A New Way of Life," *The Sign,* January, 1958.

———. "The Catholic Suburbanite." *The Sign,* February, 1958.

Harris, Chauncey. "Suburbs." *American Journal of Sociology,* July, 1943, pp. 1-13.

Harris, Louis. *Is There a Republican Majority?* New York: Harper & Brothers, 1954.

Henderson, Harry. "The Mass-Produced Suburbs, Part I." *Harper's,* November, 1953, pp. 25-32.

———. "Rugged American Collectivism, The Mass-Produced Suburbs, Part II." *Harper's,* December, 1953, pp. 80-86.

Herberg, Will. *Protestant, Catholic, Jew.* New York: Doubleday & Co., 1956.

Janosik, G. Edward. "The New Suburbia: Political Significance." *Current History,* August, 1956, pp. 91-95.

Jones, Lewis W. "The Hinterland Reconsidered." *American Sociological Review,* February, 1955, pp. 40-44.

Keats, John. *The Crack in the Picture Window.* New York: Ballantine Books, 1957.

Kitagawa, Evelyn, and Donald Bogue. *Suburbanization of Manufacturing Activities Within Standard Metropolitan Areas.* Miami, Ohio: The Scripps Foundation, 1953.

Knupfer, Genevieve. "Portrait of the Underdog." *Public Opinion Quarterly,* Spring, 1957, pp. 103-114.

Komarovsky, Mirra. "The Voluntary Associations of Urban Dwellers." *American Sociological Review,* December, 1946, pp. 686-698.

Kornhauser, Arthur, Albert J. Mayer, and Harold L. Sheppard. *When Labor Votes.* New York: University Books, 1956.

"Labor, A New Social Revolution." *Fortune,* April, 1958, pp. 215-216, 218.

Lazarsfeld, Paul, and Robert Merton. "Friendship as Social Process," in Morroe Berger, Theodore Abel, and Charles H. Page, *Freedom and Control in Modern Society.* New York: D. Van Nostrand Co., Inc., 1954, pp. 18-66.

Lerner, Max. *America as a Civilization.* New York: Simon and Schuster, 1957.

Lipset, Seymour Martin. "Trends in American Society." University of California, Berkeley, Department of Sociology and Social Institutions, 1958. Dittoed. (Relevant sections published as "What Religious Revival?" *Columbia University Forum,* Winter, 1959, pp. 12-21.)

Lowry, Ritchie. "Toward a Sociology of Suburbia." *Berkeley Publications in Society and Institutions,* Spring, 1955, pp. 12-24.

Lubell, Samuel. *The Future of American Politics.* New York: Doubleday Anchor Books, 1956.

Lundberg, George, Mirra Komarovsky, and Mary A. McInerny. *Leisure: A Suburban Study.* New York: Columbia University Press, 1934.

"The Lush New Suburban Market." *Fortune,* November, 1953, pp. 128-131, 230-237.

Lynes, Russell. *The Tastemakers.* New York: Harper & Brothers, 1954.

Martin, Walter T. "The Structuring of Social Relationships Engendered by Suburban Residence." *American Sociological Review,* August, 1956, pp. 446-453.

———. *The Rural-Urban Fringe.* Eugene: University of Oregon Press, 1953.

Mather, William G. "Income and Social Participation." *American Sociological Review,* June, 1941, pp. 380-383.

McGinley, Phyllis. "Suburbia, Of Thee I Sing." *Harper's,* December, 1949, pp. 78-82.

Mills, C. Wright. *The New Men of Power.* New York: Harcourt, Brace & Co., 1948.

Mumford, Lewis. "The Wilderness of Suburbia." *New Republic,* pp. 44-45.

"The New America: Living Atop a Civic Mushroom." *Newsweek*, April 1, 1957.

Newman, William. "Americans in Subtopia." *Dissent*, Summer, 1957, pp. 255-266.

Phillips, H. I. "The 7:58 Loses a Passenger." *Collier's*, April 11, 1925, pp. 11, 44.

Reissman, Leonard. "Levels of Aspiration and Social Class." *American Sociological Review*, June, 1953, pp. 233-242.

———. "Class, Leisure, and Social Participation." *American Sociological Review*, February, 1954, pp. 76-84.

Riesman, David. "The Suburban Dislocation." *Annals of the American Academy of Political and Social Science*, November, 1957, pp. 123-146.

Rhode, Carl von. "The Suburban Mind." *Harper's*, April, 1946, pp. 289-299.

Romanett, Raymond Paul de. "Public Action and Community Planning: A Study in the Redevelopment of Richmond, California. Unpublished master's thesis. University of California, Berkeley, Department of Sociology and Social Institutions, January, 1956.

Rosenberg, Harold. *The Tradition of the New*. New York: Horizon Press, 1959.

Rosten, Leo (ed.). *A Guide to the Religions of America*. New York: Simon and Schuster, 1955.

Rowland, Stanley, Jr. "Suburbia Buys Religion." *The Nation*, June 28, 1956, pp. 79-80.

Sayles, Leonard R. and George Strauss, *The Local Union: Its Place in the Industrial Plant*. New York: Harper & Brothers, 1953.

Schnore, Leo F. "The Functions of Metropolitan Suburbs." *American Journal of Sociology*, March, 1956, pp. 453-458.

———. "Satellites and Suburbs." *Social Forces*, December, 1957, pp. 121-127.

———. "The Growth of Metropolitan Suburbs." *American Sociological Review*, April, 1957, pp. 165-173.

Seeley, John, R. Alexander Sim, and Elizabeth Loosesley. *Crestwood Heights: A Study of the Culture of Suburban Life*. New York: Basic Books, 1956.

Shils, Edward A. "Daydreams and Nightmares: Reflections on the Criticism of Mass Culture." *Sewannee Review*, Autumn, 1957, pp. 587-608.

Spectorsky, A. C. *The Exurbanites*. Philadelphia: Lippincott, 1955.

Stein, Maurice. "Suburbia, A Walk on the Mild Side." *Dissent*, Autumn, 1957, pp. 267-275.

Swift, Ethel. "In Defense of Suburbia." *Outlook*, April 4, 1928, pp. 543-544, 558.

Tarver, James D. "Suburbanization of Retail Trade in the Standard

Metropolitan Areas of the U. S., 1948-1954." *American Sociological Review*, August, 1957, pp. 427-433.

Viereck, Peter. *Conservatism, From John Adams to Churchill.* Princeton: D. Van Nostrand Co., Inc., 1956.

Walker, C. R., and R. H. Guest. *The Man on the Assembly Line.* Cambridge: Harvard University Press, 1952.

Whetten, Nathan. "Suburbanization as a Field for Sociological Research." *Rural Sociology*, December, 1951, pp. 319-330.

Whyte, William H., Jr. "The Transients." *Fortune*, May, 1953, pp. 112-117, 221-226.

————. "The Transients, II—The Future, c/o Park Forest." *Fortune*, June, 1953, pp. 126-131, 186-196.

————. "The Transients, III—The Outgoing Life," *Fortune*, July, 1953, pp. 84-89, 160.

————. "The Transients, IV—How the New Suburbia Socializes." *Fortune*, August, 1953, pp. 120-122, 186-190.

————. *The Organization Man.* New York: Doubleday Anchor Books, 1957.

Winter, Gibson. "The Church in Suburban Captivity." *The Christian Century*, September 28, 1955, pp. 1112-1114.

Woodbury, Coleman. "Suburbanization and Suburbia." *American Journal of Public Health*, January, 1955, pp. 1-7.